A Buick
in the
Kitchen

Other Works by C.W. Gusewelle

Books
A Paris Notebook
An Africa Notebook
Quick as Shadows Passing
Far From Any Coast
A Great Current Running: The Lena River Expedition
The Rufus Chronicle: Another Autumn

Documentaries
"A Great Current Running"
"This Place Called Home"
"Water and Fire: A Story of the Ozarks"

A Buick in the Kitchen

(AND OTHER EMERGENCIES)

by

C.W. GUSEWELLE

KANSAS CITY STAR BOOKS

These essays appeared first in The Kansas City Star

Published by KANSAS CITY STAR BOOKS
1729 Grand Blvd., Kansas City, Missouri 64198

First Edition, Second Printing

Library of Congress Card Number: 00-106129

ISBN 0-9679519-2-5

Project Coordinator: Monroe Dodd
Design: Jean Donaldson Dodd
Illustrations: Hector Casanova
Dust Jacket Photograph: *The Kansas City Star*

Printed in the United States of America
by Walsworth Publishing Inc.

For Katie

TABLE OF CONTENTS

I

II

III

I

THE CLOSET PEACOCK

Grooming has never ranked high on my roster of concerns. I discontinued shaving when it became a bore. My hair — what is left of it — has been cut the same way for as long as I remember.

Clothes are of scant interest. Once every several years I am commanded by my wife and daughters to buy a suit. Choosing it takes five minutes, maybe 10. I wear it until the elbows fray or the zipper breaks. Then I get another one.

I bathe faithfully, and trim my toenails when they damage my socks. To dazzle is not my aim, even if that were possible. It would be enough if they said of me someday. "He was respectable. At least he was clean."

In this I am unlike the birds. Consider the rooster pheasant and the cock peafowl. Their voices are strident and annoying, but their plumage is spectacular and no doubt figures importantly in attracting numerous females of the breed.

I am quite the opposite. My voice can be pleasing enough when I work at it. But my wife has only to look at my misshapen flannel coat with its missing buttons to know of my absolute fidelity.

Probably there were other men, in the season of gift-giving, who asked for ornaments: diamond stickpins, studs for their cuffs, gold medallions to suspend from chains against their furred chests.

I asked for underwear.

The importance of nice underwear has been burned into my brain by the various women who have cared for me.

"What if you're in an accident?" my mother used to say.

"But I'm only 7 years old. I don't drive yet. How can I be in an accident?"

"You can't ever tell. You might be playing Kick-the-Can in the street and some crazy driver could hit you. Wouldn't that be embarrassing? You don't want to get run over wearing ratty underwear."

It was like an Eleventh Commandment, so widely understood as not to have to be carved on any stone tablet: Thou Shalt Pay Particular Attention to Thine Intimate Apparel.

Now my wife has taken over.

"How are you feeling this morning?" she may inquire obliquely as I start for the door and the car.

"Feeling? I'm feeling fine. Why, do I look queer?"

"Well, I just noticed when you were dressing that your undershirt isn't up to standard."

"What standard?"

"Hospital standard."

I explain to her that I am not going to the hospital. I am going straight to the office to spend the day with colleagues who are serious-minded men and women, and after that I am coming directly home. In that time there is apt to be little demand for me to display myself in my underwear.

"You never know. Your color hasn't been good — sort of gray. What if you have some kind of seizure?"

The grayness is a natural consequence of my age and

habits. But the power of suggestion is very strong. Feeling poorly, I drag myself back upstairs to dress for the ambulance.

Someday it will happen. I will step off the curb under the wheels of a public transit bus or will give a little sigh and topple face-forward onto my typewriter. And in my out-of-body experience, just before passing into the reported tunnel with the shining light at the end, I will look down on the shabby tenement of flesh in which I used to live.

"Stand back!" the medics will cry. "Make room! Loosen his clothing!"

My wife will be proud, then. I will be proud, too, and glad for her advice. As they draw aside the rumpled flannels and discover, with cries of surprise that the sparrow was a closet peacock after all.

"We were admiring his underwear," they will explain afterward. "And he just kind of slipped away."

LET'S CALL IT A SALAD

Our friends who visit each Christmas on their way back from Colorado always bring some remembrance of the season. One year it was an enormous spaghetti squash. Another year it was a delicious batch of homemade pesto.

This past Christmas they left with us a slender bottle of pinkish fluid, made from raspberries, its label written faintly in pencil. My wife put it on an upper cupboard shelf to be saved for a special occasion.

Time passes. The arteries harden. Eyes and the memory fail, and confusion rules.

The other evening, after the second crossword puzzle, I was overcome by a lust for ice cream. When the life force has been reduced to a barely audible hum on the encephalophone, passion of any kind is worth encouraging.

But my wife is a disciplinarian.

"Are you sure you want to do that?" she asked.

"Darned right I'm sure! I want some ice cream, and I want it now. Before I forget."

I took the carton from the freezer.

"It's more than half gone," I whined.

When all the rest has blurred, you still can recall — to the ounce — the inventory of forbidden foods.

"Somebody's been in the ice cream."

"I wouldn't know who," she said. It forever amazes me that anyone so small and innocent-appearing can be so deceitful.

But never mind. There still was enough to fill a good-sized bowl.

"What is there to put over it?" I demanded to know.

"Well," she said, "we have that nice raspberry topping our friends brought."

"Where have you hidden it?"

"On the top pantry shelf, with the bourbon." She dreams of the day when I will be unable to get up there, and then our life together will stretch ahead temperate and serene. But for a little while longer I still can reach the shelf.

I poured the pink fluid over the ice cream.

"How does it look?"

"Thin," I said. "Kind of thin."

I carried my bowl in to sit with her at the table and revel in her envy.

"I'll bet it's tasty," she said.

"Quite nice," I reported.

I took another bite.

"Well, actually . . ."

"What?" she said.

"To tell the truth, it's a little on the sour side."

"Raspberries are like that. They have an edge."

"No, I mean really sour. You can tell it's raspberry, all right. But something's gone terribly wrong."

"Maybe it's spoiled," she said. "Was it supposed to be refrigerated?"

I got the bottle down from the cupboard again, but couldn't make out the handwriting on the label.

"You have your glasses." I handed her the bottle. "What does it say?"

She got a queer look.

"It says it's raspberry vinegar."

In case you've never tried it, I can tell you that raspberry vinegar over vanilla ice cream belongs in the category of acquired tastes.

"You're not going to eat it, are you?"

"It's the last of the ice cream. I can't just throw it out."

We're all prisoners of our past, and I was raised at a table where waste was an unpardonable sin.

"But it might make you sick!"

"If I think of it as a salad," I told her, "I believe I can keep it down."

ON BORROWED TIME

S he came to us from the street, and we know which year she joined our house. The question is whether the old dog is 20 now, or only 19.

About five years ago, I think it was, I wrote a piece saying how that would be her last autumn. She rallied, though, and greeted another spring.

Then there was some further crisis. I wrote her under again, and again she made a comeback. This happened three or four times. I'm a little gun-shy on the subject.

"I remember a column about that old dog you used to have," someone will say. "I'll bet you hated to lose her."

"Well, as a matter of fact —"

"What was that dog's name?"

"Cinnamon."

"That's it. It's been so long I'd forgotten."

"To be perfectly honest about it —"

"I had a dog once that lived to be 14. They get to be like family."

"They sure do. But about old Cinnamon —"

"I had a friend say once she'd sooner put her husband to sleep than the dog."

The best thing then is just to let it go and try to change the subject. Credibility's at stake. It's like when a boat goes down, the funeral is held and the dead man is found a couple of years later living the sweet life under a different name in Argentina. People don't like to hear they've grieved for nothing.

The truth is, though, she's still with us.

She can't see, can't hear and has trouble getting around. She had a stroke last year, and to watch her cross a room is to be reminded that the terra isn't any too firma — that we really do live on a round object spinning at a great rate on its axis.

This year, somehow, she broke a wrist. If walking's a trick on four legs, how can it be managed on three? We gave her up again.

Our friend, the veterinarian, tried binding her wrist in a removable cast. She's his oldest patient, and healing would be uncertain and slow, he said. If it didn't work, we'd have a decision to make. At some point, for her sake, enough hurting would be enough.

But she mended. And divides her days, now, between the fenced yard when it's bright and warm, and her rug in the corner of the kitchen when it's not.

The geography of the house is clear in her memory. She knows where the water bowl should be, and the turns of the doorways, and all the places where the sun through the windows makes a warm spot on the floor.

Her friends, the cats, come around her and sometimes touch noses. Carried up the stairs at night, she prefers to eat from the bird dog's bowl and grumbles if he takes too much.

She's gotten so gray and fine and light — light as a leaf that could ride away on the autumn wind. But she knows us by our scents, and comes beside the chair, lifting her head to be touched. And, being touched, she smiles.

Each morning we look to see if she is breathing. She's made a fraud of me enough times already, so I risk no more predictions. We and she just take her borrowed days as they come.

GENERATIONS

Like flint points in the layered earth of some forgotten camp, the artifacts of modern lives are deposited in high cupboards, so far beyond the hand's or the memory's reach that exhuming them is a kind of domestic archaeology.

We only intended to have the kitchen painted. But painting was the least of it. First, all the shelves had to be emptied, their contents packed in boxes and carried to another room. Then the whole operation had to be repeated in exact reverse.

A considerable labor, it turned out to be: wife washing and polishing, one daughter helping hand the objects up, and me perched on a tall stool, reaching to set them in their places, not to be seen again until — how long? Another decade or two?

"It's crazy," our daughter said.

"What is?"

"So many glasses and cups and plates. We never use half of it. Why keep it all?"

We didn't really answer. Some things are unexplainable. We just kept passing the bits of memory from careful hand to hand.

The small maroon dish of knobby glass, for instance. Not a thing of any value, just a dish like any other. But, holding it, I remembered suddenly from childhood the place it occupied on the table beside a lamp. And how for most of the year it might contain a thimble, stray safety pins or other oddments, but always at Christmas it filled up with the bright, hard candies I never learned to like.

Forty years ago was like yesterday. I saw the room in every detail, and my parents in their chairs, younger than I am now.

"You keep things because you have to," I said, and put the maroon dish on a top shelf.

"Not me," our daughter said. "I won't have a clutter of stuff."

"Well, that's your business."

"I won't," she said again. "Plates to eat from, glasses to drink from. Only the things I really need and use. Life ought to be simple."

"Yes," I said, "I used to think so. But it never is."

To nearly everything some name attached. A slender vase that once held a single bud. The giver of that, and the occasion, were remembered. A pretty teacup with the handle broken. A music box that, when wound, sang out again the merry tune that used to fill the nursery.

At least three generations' gatherings were represented. Maybe four. My wife was from a family of savers. Grandmother, mother, widowed aunts and maiden ones long gone, cousins several times removed — all filling cupboards that have emptied finally, like tributaries, into ours.

We have imagined, from time to time, that when the girls were grown it would be simpler to live in an apartment. But this project of the kitchen has made clear the utter foolishness of that.

"We're here for good," I said from my perch on the shaky stool. "After that it's your problem. Yours and your sister's."

The river runs on through us to them, freighted with nearly forgotten things, collecting as it goes. For an odd moment I could see my daughter, in some place of her own. Suddenly she was our age, with her ideas changed, her dream of simplicity worn down and lost. She was taking things from cupboards and putting them back again, remembering this exact day in the house of her own girlhood, speaking names.

Then the image faded, and she was young again.

"It's pretty," she said, looking at a painted bowl. "Pretty things should be used."

"That was your grandmother's," her mother said. "Or it might have come from Aunt Crete."

Passed up to me, it sank away again into the layers of lost time where it will wait with the potsherds and shaped flints and antique hearths — unseen, unspoken of — until another shift of diggers comes with spades and sifting screens to turn the ancient ground.

OOZING CHARM

We feel a little flush of pleasure when people speak of the charm of old houses. Ours is, by every calculation, old.

Driving home late the other evening, we spoke of the preparations that still needed to be made for guests coming for a family gathering the next noon. The house had been tidied, and beverages stocked. All that remained was the cooking.

Our visiting daughter had come in first and met us at the door.

"I'm sorry to have to tell you," she said, "but I'm afraid there's been an attack of charm. The kitchen sink won't drain."

"Not at all?"

"I tried the plunger, but it didn't help."

"No," I said, "that's no use." I knew that from having been charmed several times before in the area of the kitchen sink.

We sank into chairs, in that state of temporary paralysis often induced by such news. We looked at one another, and at the sink. I imagined our guests arriving on the morrow, convivial and expectant — then being driven to their knees by the miasma of putrescence emitting from the clogged drain.

"We'll take them to a deli," said my wife.

Time passed while we considered that.

"Or . . ." I said.

"Or what?"

"We could call a plumber." I do not respond well in emergencies. It had taken most of an hour to arrive at that novel strategy.

She looked in the phone book and found several that offered 24-hour service. It was a busy night, and all the crews were engaged. The earliest a man could come was between 1 and 2 a.m.

"I'll wait up while he fixes it," I said.

At the stroke of 1 o'clock the plumber arrived. Mike was his name, and he'd been at it since 7 a.m. the previous day. His manner at the start was brisk and optimistic. But two attempts with the mechanical snake did not open the drain.

So some of the fittings under the sink were sawed out and replaced. Still the water did not flow.

I was reminded of once in a dentist's office when things went terribly wrong and the dentist lost his composure and began to cry, and I was afraid he would just give up and go home and leave me there in the chair. It crossed my mind something like that could happen to Mike.

Then, a little after 3 o'clock, we both got a kind of second wind.

"The block's farther down," he said.

"Maybe in the standpipe." I was just guessing at the nomenclature, but miraculously got it right.

"Could be. Let's have a look."

"I hate for you to go down to the basement."

"Listen," he said, "I've seen some basements."

The snake whirled and rattled inside the standpipe. He ran the thing out 50 feet. The house vibrated. A light went on in the neighbor's upstairs bedroom.

"Surely that's cleared it."

"Surely," I said. "Let's call it a night."

It was getting on toward 24 hours since either of us had slept, and the brief adrenaline rush had passed. It was half-past 5 o'clock. Another hour and the sky would start to pale.

Mike sat for several minutes under the dome light of his van, writing out the bill. They say there are some things you can't put a price on, but charm is not one of them.

He wrote his phone number on the top of the bill.

"Any more problems, just give me a call."

There are more problems, of course — the thousand-year-old furnace, the low pressure in a second-floor faucet, the commode that runs all the time.

I didn't speak of those, though. He'd been determined, and had stuck with the job to the end. But he had the look of a man who'd gone the limit, and who might not much care to discuss the further charms of old houses.

A BUICK IN THE KITCHEN

Some people are forever asking why men can't take on a fairer share of the duties around the house. Why, for instance, can't men help with the cooking?

I'll tell you why. It's because their wives are too big.

We live in a normal-size house, and now, with the children grown and gone for most of the year, there is ample space for the two of us. We are smallish people, my wife and I, and thus are able to pass freely up and down stairs and from room to room without running into one another.

Everywhere except in the kitchen.

It's a regular sort of kitchen, with counters, appliances, a telephone table and enough floor space for eight or 10 people to stand around comfortably talking, as they sometimes do while waiting for me to pour out their ration of cheer.

But let me go in there planning to cook something, and immediately my wife comes in after me and inflates.

In her normal configuration she is only a little more than 5 feet tall and petite as a schoolgirl, and you would not think someone like that could swell up large enough to fill a whole kitchen. It's an amazing trick, but she does it every time.

If I need to use the tap of the sink, she is there, already using it. There was no indication beforehand that she planned to be working in the kitchen at all, but there she is, blocking my way.

All right, I tell myself. Let her finish whatever she's doing at the sink. I will just get what I need from the refrigerator.

So I start to turn in the other direction, but she is there, too, the refrigerator door already open and positioned so it is impossible to get around her.

Well, I think, at least I can get out a pan from the cupboard so that, if the traffic ever clears, I will be ready to go forward.

That's hopeless, though. Because by now she has achieved her full expansion, and there is no longer even a dream of making my way to the cupboard.

I really can't say what accounts for this phenomenon. We are territorial creatures, and it may be that wives — even ones who profess to despise cooking — resent any encroachment on their turf, in the same way certain groups will fight to the death over a scrap of land whose only virtue is that it is theirs.

All I know is that there is no use trying to do any useful work while sharing a kitchen with a wife half-again larger than a 1957 Buick.

So at this point, after several violent collisions, I usually let out a little groan and give the whole thing up, withdraw to a chair somewhere and pick up a magazine or newspaper that is sure to contain another article about how much better and fairer the world would be if only men would do their share.

I am all for breaking down the gender barriers.

For example, I am careful not to get in her way, or interfere in any fashion, when my wife is doing the yard work. Did I complain when she took over the traditional male tasks of household repairs, hauling out the trash, cleaning the gutters?

No. Not a murmur. And yet, after all these concessions on my part, the kitchen remains hers.

I say that if society is to evolve in the way the militants want it to, there's going to have to be a little reciprocal consideration from the other side.

THE SECRET LODGER

Her urgent whisper came to me through the fog of sleep. I wasn't sure I'd heard right.

"Someone did what?" I mumbled.

"Someone just flushed the downstairs toilet."

That was arresting news to receive at half past 3 o'clock in the morning — especially since we're the only two people who live here. At least we think we are.

"Maybe it was a cat," I said.

"Don't be silly. Cats use litter boxes. Whoever heard of a cat flushing a toilet?"

"Well, what do you want me to do?"

"Check it out, that's what! It might be a prowler."

"Can't it wait until morning?"

"No," she said. "Now."

I listened at the top of the stair. There was no sound of furtive movement below. Then I went down to check out the doors and windows. Everything was closed and locked.

"No one's gotten in," I reported.

"Well, I know what I heard. It did flush."

It was a bafflement. The only explanation I could think of was that we had a secret lodger — someone who hid in the basement, or in the crawl space under the back room, slipping out into the house at night to attend to sanitary needs.

It was an unsettling notion. I wondered how long he might have been with us. Only days? Or could it have been years? Then there was another flush. And this one I heard, too.

"It's times like these when homeowners need guns," I said.

"That's going a little overboard, isn't it?"

"Not at all," I told her. "A man's house is his castle. He has a right to defend the throne."

"Surely you wouldn't shoot someone just for using the toilet," she said.

"People have been shot for less."

"Yes," she said, "and I remember reading about a man who shot his mother-in-law in the garage at night because he said he thought she was a raccoon. It was a terrible mistake."

"Maybe. Maybe not."

This time I descended the stair noisily, turning on lights as I went, hurling my empty bluff ahead of me: "I'm warning whoever's there! I will plug the first man who moves!"

I looked in the hall closet, under tables. I opened all the kitchen cupboards on the chance an intruder might have folded himself inside. I even ventured down with a flashlight into the dungeon of a basement.

Again, there was no one.

"Then it must be the phantom flush," my wife said.

"Beg pardon?"

"I heard someone speak of it once. The thing goes off without any explanation. It's one of life's big mysteries."

That sounded screwy, so the next morning I telephoned a plumbing contractor who confirmed there really was such a phenomenon. He said they get calls all the time about phantom flushes.

"It's a leaky valve in the flush box," he told me. "Bring the mechanism in and we'll fix or replace it."

I thanked him and hung up. I am ungifted at plumbing and wouldn't dream of taking our toilet apart. Zoning prohibits backyard privies, and it's too far to walk to an all-night convenience store.

By amazing coincidence, that very day's paper had a toilet story. It told about a restaurant patron in Indiana who got upset because the stool in the restroom flushed too slowly, so he whipped out his pistol and blew the fixture apart.

"They must allow concealed carry in Indiana," I said.

"I don't know," said my wife. "But I think it goes to show that toilets and guns don't mix."

ANNIVERSARY

We were young in a simpler — some might say a more priggish — time. She is the only woman I have ever lived with, or ever mean to. But that has not seemed an arid design for a life, nor has it seemed like so many years.

There was a drafty cottage at the edge of the country, where the pipes froze in winter and where, that first summer, the stone-walled pond was grand for swimming in.

Then there was a proper house in town, with a fireplace in which we cooked the ducks I shot, a small and sometimes fruitful dooryard garden, a screened porch on which we sat to feel the seasons change.

Friends filled that house with the kind of spendthrift joy — languorous and unguarded — that people have before they know the heartbreaks coming. I can remember how young, how untroubled, their faces were, seen across a table or reflected in a mirror.

Upstairs there was a sunny room in which her mother passed the last years with us. And just along the hall from that, the nursery in which our daughters spent their earliest ones. Their first adventure was to creep into that other room, that other bed, and, bundled under blankets there, share an old woman's cache of soda crackers at an hour when all else was mysterious and still.

Finally, there is the present house, a congenial place, but in some odd way never quite as completely ours as that first one was.

So that has been the geography of our lives. And, again, it is fairly simple — compared, that is, to the more elaborate histories of people who change homes, change cities, with a rootless facility. Sheer restlessness propels them, or ambition does. They are experts at moving, but forever amateurs at staying.

From each of those two previous places I took away memories. Not just generalized recollections, but small memories, specific and distinct. I remember a particular moment in a certain room — the quality of light, the exact words said, the positions of the speakers, and how their faces looked.

The country cottage is a ruin now. When I went there for the last time ever, the windows had been broken out and a part of the ceiling had fallen. The place had been bedded in by drifters who had written furious and crazed graffiti on our walls.

The house where the nursery was, and her mother's room, has since been occupied by two sets of different people. The first ones walled up the screened porch to make a room, thrust out as ungainly as a goiter at the side. The second bunch painted the whole exterior a nasty yellow. I have to turn my head away when I pass that street.

Still, in my mind, the cottage and the house are exactly as they used to be. And the memories I keep are of things that happened last week, last year or at most the year before. They are peopled by friends as hopeful and untroubled as friends used to be.

But memory is false.

Between that first spring and this one, we have, like anyone, had lives to live. And occupations to pursue, in the usual combination of elation and rage. And awful losses to endure — meaning by that the losses of people, since no other kind has lasting power to hurt.

And we have changed. The striving — because that's the nature of most lives — has left us less playful than I seem to think we used to be. We are more fixed in our notions, and at the same time less certain of anything.

Sometimes, in the morning, I splash water on my face and look up with real astonishment at the stranger staring back at me from the glass. Whose wreck is that? And how depressing for the girl who must wake up beside it in the bed.

Thirty-four years it's been in all. And for that anniversary the manuals of social grace have no suggestions to make.

Six is for iron. Eight is for bronze and eleven for steel.

The precious metals — platinum and silver and gold — all fall in years divisible by five. For 34, nothing is mentioned.

The best we can give each other, it appears, is a few more years in the refining heat of the fire, to see what substance this brief affair was made of, after all.

GROOVING THE SWING

You never know when life is going to take an ugly turn. Or which direction bad luck will hit you from.

Drugs I've managed to escape. Gambling's not a sickness. Rampant lechery, beyond a certain age, sounds like a lot of work. What's happened in recent weeks is that I've fallen deeply into golf.

It's a contemptible addiction, and I used to think it couldn't happen to me. That's what they all think. But I went to a garage sale, and found a set of clubs for about the price of a restaurant dinner. And the rot set in.

I went out with those clubs and scored 102, which for a serious golfer would be a catastrophe, but for me was shining triumph. A couple of days later I went out again. That time it took only 94 strokes to get around the course.

I have begun to dream the game. Golf dreams are better than erotic dreams, because they last all night. The map of the fairways and greens is perfectly clear in my mind. Dreaming, I am able to play in fewer strokes than when awake — usually between 65 and 75. When evening comes on, I can hardly wait to lie down and tee up the ball.

My wife has noticed the change that's come over me.

"You're sleeping a lot," she said. "Are you sick?"

"No, I'm practicing."

"You're what?"

"I'm practicing," I told her. "Golf is a mental game."

"I don't mean to be snide and carping," she said. "But I always thought golf was played outdoors, in the daytime."

"Not championship golf," I told her. "At my level, championship golf is played in bed. You have to be able to visualize the shots before you can hit them."

"I thought you were just sleeping. That shows how much I know about it."

"Tonight, for example, I am going to play a par-three, 195-yard hole over water. When I am awake, it is three lost balls in the lake and a 12. But in my dreams, when I visualize it, it's a nice 5-iron about six feet from the pin."

"Congratulations," she said.

"Thanks, but one hole doesn't make a round."

Eventually, the time comes when you have to put all this practice to work on a real course. I went out with a friend, and played the first three holes in par, par and birdie. It was just like a dream.

Then I realized it wasn't a dream. That made me nervous and I lost my concentration. The whole thing came apart. I had to take vacation and spend a week in bed, visualizing, just to repair the damage to my game.

After the mental aspect, the next most important part is equipment. My golfing friend says that playing in tennis shoes is a handicap, and that real golf shoes with spikes would gain me four or five strokes, minimum.

"If you wear shoes with spikes to bed," my wife said, "one of us is going to sleep on the couch."

She put her magazine on the bedside table and switched off the light. "You heard what I said, didn't you?"

"Shhhh," I told her. "You don't speak while someone is lining up a putt."

"It sure is lonely around here," she said.

"Golf," I told her, "is the loneliest game in the world."

KING OF THE LINKS

A golf course just before dawn is a magical place.

The clubhouse is dark. No cars are in the parking lot. The last stars glitter overhead. A powerful scent of verdancy fills the air. But the course itself — the undulations of the fairways, the thickets of ball-eating trees, the rank grass of the waste areas — can only be sensed, not seen.

There is a wonderful stillness, as on a battlefield before the warring armies wake. No tragic blows have yet been struck.

We'd agreed to meet early, at the course where I've been misspending a little time, to see if we might get in a round before noon. Six o'clock was the hour agreed, but I woke up early, impatient for this chance to dishonor myself, and got there at 20 minutes past 5.

The golf course dog and I were the only creatures stirring. Teddy, I think I've heard him called.

I was standing in the coolness, listening to the car radio play some country tune about betrayal and a broken heart, when Teddy sauntered down from his station outside the snack bar to see which of the pitiful, demented human souls it was who'd shown up first this day.

He came with a fine sense of proprietorship, the way a farmer strides down across his field to find out what trespasser he's heard shooting quail in one of his coverts.

Teddy's a black Labrador, or mostly that, gone heavy in the middle and with a bit of the old-age stiffness coming on him, as it does with us all.

I gave a whistle, but he wasn't interested in being petted. He had a whole day of that ahead of him, and didn't see any point in starting early.

He just checked me out from a distance of several steps. With great deliberation, he watered a bush. Then he set off on his morning rounds. Over to the practice range first, to be sure the grass was growing as it should and was ready for the assaults of the hackers.

Then back up to the putting green, to have a look at where the cups were cut. Then down toward the first tee, to verify the markers were in place and the towel was hanging from the ball washer, as it ought to be.

The eastern sky was lightening now. And having done what he could to be sure the day was starting correctly, he returned to his spot outside the snack bar to wait for the people to come.

Teddy knows golfers. He's seen them by the tens of thousands — arriving with their quick, hopeful steps, voices bright with optimism. And stumbling back in several hours later, stammering, shoulders slumped, humiliated in ways he is glad not to have watched.

There are iron tables on the patio, and sometimes, in fatigue and brokenness, the people are careless with their potato chips and Polish sausages. And Teddy accepts these little accidents as they come — although he prefers the regular sausages to the spicy kind.

I'm not much given to envy. I don't envy my friends, Ernie and Art, the way their iron shots fly high and straight, or how, on days when the wind is right, they aim straight across the big pond toward the green on No. 8, while I, in feebleness and fear, take three strokes to skirt the shoreline.

But I envy Teddy.

He spends all his time at that pretty place. He never shanked a ball, or hit one off the toe. He never found an unplayable lie. His handicap is zero, and every day turns out pretty much as he'd planned.

The game, the way I play it, yields mostly sadness. In the next life, I'd rather be the golf course dog.

STUCK IN ACT THREE

The performance had been enjoyable. Cries of "Bravo!" rained down on the stage, and we stood with the rest of the audience to applaud the players as they took their bows.

People started filing into the aisles. I would have followed them, except my leg was stuck to the upturned seat.

Some prognathous goon had disposed of a monstrous chaw of bubble gum — about a six-piece wad of the stuff — by affixing it to the underside of the theater seat. The gum had bonded to my trouser leg, holding me in place.

I jerked free, pulling half the wad with me, pink strings

of it hanging down toward my shoe.

"Stay clear!" I cried, warning the people around me. "Don't anyone come near. I am unclean!"

We made our way to the theater foyer, the pant leg heavy and stiff against my calf. My wife, who is ingenious in such matters, found ice in a cooler behind the refreshment counter, froze the gum hard and managed to chip off the greater part — enough of it, anyhow, that I could drive home without fouling the car.

I decided, then, that I am what the egalitarian death squads like to call a cultural elitist.

Actually, I had begun to sense this tendency in myself as early as Act I, when two women in the next row forward were sharing a pair of opera glasses, passing them back and forth from one to the other.

The younger one had a head of hair roughly the size of a state-fair-champion pumpkin. Every time she gave or received the glasses, she lurched violently to the side, that enormous head blocking the view of the stage completely. She did this about every five minutes during the evening.

My cultural elitism worsened during Act II, when the woman to my immediate left was seized by a fit of sneezing, projecting advanced civilizations of bacteria over everyone within range of her nose.

Then, at the end, came the gum.

Taken together, these experiences produced what is known in the language of the theater as a willing suspension of civility.

Immediately upon reaching home and getting out of my gum-crusted trousers, I sat down to write out a few simple rules which, if the authority were mine, would be enforced at all musical performances, stage plays or other elitist cultural events.

* Any woman appearing at the theater wearing a bouf-fant hairstyle would be given the choice of having her head shaved to the scalp or participating in mud-wrestling events at the annual stag parties of men's clubs with the names of animals.

* Persons of either gender attempting to attend a performance while exhibiting symptoms of a cold would be removed to a sterile holding area for examination by an independent panel of ear, nose and throat specialists. Those determined to be in an actively contagious state would be barred for life from all public spectacles except rock concerts, beauty pageants and tractor pulls.

* Individuals found with chewing gum, or related paraphernalia, within 500 yards of any place of entertainment would be charged with reckless endangerment and unlawful possession, and would have their teeth forcibly extracted on the spot.

At a time when two tickets in the balcony can set you back the equivalent of a week's wage, these precautions seem to me altogether moderate and reasonable. If that's elitism, make the most of it.

Legends of the Tribe

A notice in yesterday's mail brought word of a wonderful new book that can be mine on request — provided the request is accompanied by a check or money order. But I must act now, or lose this chance forever.

The title of the book is *Gusewelles Across America.*

All right, maybe it isn't The Kennedys of Massachusetts, but still it has a certain sweep. Across America! Gusewelles girdling the continent! Can you imagine that?

According to the order form, this book is the result of research involving thousands, perhaps even millions, of official documents — including, I would suppose, penitentiary inmate rosters and records of assorted army desertions and bankruptcies.

It comes hard-bound, with gold-stamped lettering on an imitation leather cover, and will be published in a special limited edition. A very limited edition. In fact, fewer than 15 copies will be produced, all on special order, which suggests to me either that the number of Gusewelles able to read is fairly small or that their salting across America is exceedingly thin.

It is the work, evidently, of a woman named Mary Whitney in Ottsville, Pa. At least she's the one to whom the money is supposed to be sent. And what use would I find for such a book? For one thing, Ms. Whitney tells me, it will "aid in the study of the Gusewelle migrations and settlements in America with geographic counts." For another, it will "help to initiate relationships with other Gusewelle families."

Maybe so, but I'm pretty much one for letting sleeping dogs lie.

While I have no hard data on the matter, I have always rather imagined the Gusewelle "migrations and settlements" to be events better described as hasty flights punctuated by brief periods of squatting. Maybe that is all wrong. Maybe, sometime during the perambulations of our clan, there was a Gusewelle who escaped his destiny as a hewer of wood and carrier of water and made a big success (if not a famous name) for himself. If so, he didn't mention me in his will.

As for establishing contact with distant and unknown relations, it's a risk I'd as soon not take. Once in a great while I write my daughters, who are off somewhere in school. But that's about all the commerce in Gusewelles I'm good for.

My wife is related on both sides of her family to Daniel Boone. Somehow word of that got circulated. Now we wake up with night sweats, expecting at any time two or three members of the Boone Society — or maybe a couple of dozen of them — will appear on the doorstep with their suitcases, planning to stay about a year.

A bunch of Boones would be nightmare enough. I'm just not up to a gang of Gusewelles.

Also, I'm an orderly man. I hate confusions. Several years ago a fellow in another city — a Gusewelle with the same first name and middle initial as mine, and exactly my age — was killed in an automobile accident. The story came in on the news wire and one of the editors carried it over, ashen faced, and asked me how I felt. My wife was most of a month answering the sympathy notes.

I'm not saying that *Gusewelles Across America* isn't a beauty. Or that it isn't literature. But $29.85 is more than I'm in the habit of paying for a book I haven't seen and isn't even printed yet.

I've decided to wait for the reviews.

II

THEY'RE EATING THE ICE!

I am not at home in famous and wickedly expensive restaurants, which is as it should be. Since all restaurant food tastes very much the same to me, it is only by being intimidated and made to feel oafish and provincial that I can be sure I have spent my money wisely, rubbing shoulders with the heavy hitters.

The other night, several of us gathered in such a place to celebrate the birthday of a friend.

Shortly a man appeared and, with a flourish, placed before us a bowl of crushed ice with forks thrust in it. The habitués of that establishment would have called the waiter by name, and perhaps complimented him on the coldness of the forks — which were for the salad that had not yet arrived.

But our faces fell in disappointment. We thought that, in order to blend in with the heavy hitters, we were going to be expected to sit around the table making small talk and eating ice.

One of our group had arrived early and had dispensed the intelligence that it cost 75 cents to check a coat, payable on demand. So we kept our wraps with us, folded beside us in the booth. The various table attendants noticed that. They kept looking at our coats as if we had tracked something in on our shoes.

The dinner was very elegant. I knew it was elegant

because there were several things on the plate I could not identify. Others had the same problem. And after the business with the ice we were jumpy. We did not want to cut up and eat something that might turn out afterward to be part of the decor.

The meal lasted a long time. It makes no sense, when you have gotten dressed up and paid to park, to eat and run. Midway in the evening it was necessary to excuse myself from the table for an errand common to us all.

In the men's room I noticed a man coming suddenly at me out of the corner. I whirled and threw up my fists and faced that dude, ready for any funny business. It turned out he only wanted to rent me a towel. The heavy hitters find paper towels unsatisfactory. They have to have people to hand them their linens and shine their shoes. Using the restroom becomes a team affair, requiring extensive personnel. When a restaurant brings you forks in a bowl of ice, you can be pretty sure that they will recoup in the toilet.

It is like a bus station. Either you have a quarter in your pocket or you are in for a long, uncomfortable evening.

The food was fine. There wasn't a lot of it, but what there was seemed nourishing. We had trouble during the evening getting ice in our water glasses. The waiter would have preferred to pour wine. But we finally got the hang of it. We would complain to the waiter that our forks had gotten hot, and when he came with the bowl of ice we would use that for our water.

Finally a whisper went around the table. Who was going to ask for separate checks? There were 10 of us. The waiters were looking at our coats and fully expecting that we would ask for separate checks — being fairly certain by now that we were not heavy hitters.

We surprised them. One of the wives paid the whole thing with a credit card. A credit card is the next best thing to being a heavy hitter. Don't leave home without it.

The rest of us stood around then, shaking the folds out of our coats, doing long division and writing dubious personal bank drafts to the one who had paid the bill.

The management got nervous again. They brought roses for the ladies. Some of the ladies put the roses in their hair. Others affixed them to strategic areas of their dresses. I didn't get a rose. What I wanted to ask for, if I'd had the nerve, was a free pass to the restroom.

The maitre d' was suave as a seal.

"Come back," he said. "Sometime."

THE TROPHY CAT

The trophy cat, Teddy, is on a diet, and it's a trial for everyone in the house. He did not choose this thorny path of self-improvement. Who ever does? He was forced to walk it.

"Do you know how much Teddy weighs?" our daughter asked.

"Twenty-three pounds," I replied. "The size of a supermarket frozen turkey, more or less."

"More."

"Well, that was his last weigh-in — 23, right on the mark."

"It's 26 now."

"Good. Only four more to go. I would like to be able to say I once owned a 30-pound cat."

"He's put on three more pounds in a year."

"That's not so much," I said.

"Are you kidding? At that rate, in five years he'll weigh more than the bird dog."

"Teddy is big-boned," my wife put in. "He carries it well."

The truth is, he rarely carries it at all. Mostly he puts it in a chair and leaves it there. His legs have all but disappeared.

"The diet starts tomorrow," our daughter declared flatly. "There's special food for cats with a severe eating disorder like his."

"It can't be done," we protested. "What about all the other cats?"

"We'll figure out a way," she said.

And we have, sort of. But it is incredibly complicated. They are used to eating, all of them, at bowls arranged on the kitchen counter. Now we have to segregate them. The trouble is that several of them have learned to open the kitchen door.

So when the others are eating, Teddy's food bowl is on the floor in the outer hall and the door is secured with heavy rubber bands. Lest he sink into deep depression, it is necessary from time to time to carry his bowl back to the counter so he may take nourishment in the familiar place, and to put theirs on the floor outside.

Teddy is disgusted by his slimming ration, although it is the same in shape and texture as the regular food, differing only slightly in color.

The others, noticing the special treatment he is receiving, naturally have decided that his food is uncommonly desirable, and they miss no opportunity to poach at his bowl.

No matter which food is on the floor in the hall, it lies in the immediate trajectory of the bird dog, Rufus, on his careens between the back yard and the chair in the upstairs bedroom. And Rufus considers both brands superior to his own, although three of the cats would prefer to eat dog food if they were allowed.

The management of all this is like one of those thought problems that used to defeat me in grade school arithmetic. My wife or I spend a good deal of time closed up in the kitchen, shouting out into the house for the other to come take the rubber bands off the door.

But it seems to be paying off. He is down three pounds, to 23 again, and last night we noticed that Teddy's legs had reappeared. We have begun to detect flatter places at the sides, although the impression he gives still is largely spherical.

And best of all, he is markedly more active. We're apt to see him now almost anywhere in the house. Yesterday he was upstairs several times.

I wouldn't exactly say he frolics. His brow is furrowed. He moves with purpose. He knows we're operating at the very edge of our administrative competence, and that sometime, somewhere, we'll make a mistake with the bowls.

A KNOBBY PROBLEM

"We have to sell the house," I told my wife.

"What's happened?" she wanted to know. "Did you go to the casino? Have you been fired, or what?"

"We just can't live here anymore, that's all. We have to sell."

"You said that. I want a reason."

"The doorknobs," I whined. "They come off in your hand."

"That's it — the whole thing? The doorknobs?"

"It's enough," I said. "You go in a room, and the knob comes off. There you are, standing there holding it, and you never know if you'll be able to get out again."

"But didn't we pay a man to fix them?"

"It doesn't matter. They still come off."

"All of them?"

"No, not all. But the ones that don't come off you have to fiddle with to make the door latch at all."

"You shouldn't get so worked up," she said.

"Who's worked up? Listen, I spent my whole boyhood in a modest little bungalow. There was a big depression. Times were hard. There wasn't any extra money. But at least the knobs stayed on the doors."

"Your father probably kept them working."

"Not a chance!" I said. "He was a fine man, but he was not gifted with his hands."

"It's genetic then."

"What's that supposed to mean?"

"Nothing. I'm sure you could fix those knobs if you wanted to."

"Yes," I said. "If I wanted to. And if I had the tools."

"You had a screwdriver once."

"I know, but it's gotten away somewhere. And what's the use, anyway? Fix the doorknobs, and the faucet washers go. Replace those, and ceiling lights burn out. It's endless," I declared. "The place is just wearing out and running down."

"Before we pack up and move," she said, "what if I just call another man to try to fix the knobs?"

"And change the washers? And replace the lights?"

"Why not?" she said. "It's worth a try."

"All right. We can have one more crack at it. But if the knobs still aren't right, we're out of here."

"To where?" she said. "Maybe the country? We could have a barn with a hundred cats."

"I suppose so."

"And since nobody in the country locks the house, we could leave the doors open, and knobs wouldn't matter."

"Right."

"And you could have a workshop. You could get power tools and take up crafts. You might even overcome your handicap about working with your hands."

I said nothing.

"Somehow, you don't look excited about that."

"Not especially," I said.

"Well, what did you have in mind?"

"To be perfectly honest, I was thinking more along the lines of a nice motel."

"Come out of your office," she said, "and we'll have

lunch and talk about it."

"That's the problem," I told her. "I can't."

This room where I work has a door with glass panes, and she looked through the glass at the knob I was holding.

"All right," she said. "Then I'll see what I can slide under the door."

TALKING HOUSES

The other evening, at about the supper hour, I heard what sounded like a noisy conversation in the front yard. So I stepped outside to see who was there.

No one was in sight. Yard and street were empty. It turned out to be one of the houses on the block talking.

Burglary! Burglary! the house was saying.

Woooo-ah! Whooo-ah! Burglary! Burglary! You have entered an area protected by a security alarm. Leave the premises immediately!

The words were clear as anything on the cold night air. Having never before heard a talking house, I headed up the street to see which one it was that had discovered the power of speech.

The police already had arrived. No sign of forced entry had been found, they said. Evidently the people who live there had gone out for the evening and left a door ajar. And the house, noticing this, had begun to vocalize.

Burglary! it was shouting. *Woooo-ah! Burglary! Burglary! Leave the premises immediately!*

The officers were trying to locate on the telephone someone who knew how to tell the house that it had made a mistake. They must have succeeded, because after while the shouting stopped.

It got me thinking, though, about this whole new subject of talking houses, and the wonderful range of possibilities it opens up. Reason says that once a house is able to talk it need not be limited to announcing burglaries. It could be programmed to say almost anything.

Get your dog off the grass! Woooo-ah! You have 10 seconds to get off the grass before the electric grid is activated.

Or perhaps:

Shut off the lawn mower! It is 7 o'clock on a Saturday morning and your neighbors are trying to sleep. Woooo-ah! Shut off the lawn mower immediately or it will be confiscated.

Or possibly:

You have entered an area where soliciting and proselytizing are prohibited. Do not touch the door bell. Warning, the door bell is fully armed! Depart forthwith!

The possibilities are endless. What's appealing is the fine impersonality of the announcements. You would not be saying those things. Your *house* would be saying them, thus enabling you to avoid giving offense to neighbors, dog-walkers, candy-sellers and cruising evangelists.

Many years ago I read a story that I think was by Ray Bradbury, though I cannot find it in my collection of his work, so I may be giving him credit for someone else's story.

Anyway, it was about a city of the future after all the people were gone. I don't recall whether they'd left for somewhere else, or vanished in some catastrophe. But in any case the city was abandoned.

However, the fully automated houses kept going through their routines — issuing wake-up calls, brewing coffee, making breakfast, then throwing out the uneaten food, tidying themselves up, preparing lunch, and so forth. Repeating it all endlessly, or until civilization's batteries ran down.

I thought of that story as I walked back through the chilly dark after hearing the house up the street announce an encroachment upon itself.

And I wondered what it would be like when all the other houses had learned to talk, and were shouting their bulletins and warnings back and forth to one another, with no living ear to listen and no one to shut them off.

It's the gift of science fiction writers to imagine almost everything before it happens. Now that's the unsettling part.

MAKE MINE SUNNY SIDE UP

Jack London or some other chronicler of the far north, in describing winter in the Klondike, once wrote of cold so terrible that, if a man spat, his spittle would freeze and crack with a report like a pistol shot before it hit the ground.

Now that is cold.

It may also be hyperbole, although I can't say — never having passed a winter at the correct latitude for explosive spitting.

You have heard the expression, "So hot you could fry an egg on the sidewalk." That, too, has descriptive vigor. But it is empty of truth. Eggs will not fry on the sidewalk. I say that on the basis of empirical evidence. I tried it the other day.

The digital thermometer on the front of one bank read 100 degrees. Another read 107. The radio said 103. Cats stood motionless in the shadow of larger dogs. Birds stood in the shadow of the cats. Caterpillars sought out the shade of birds. People coming out of air-conditioned offices staggered and went to their knees.

How hot was it? It was so hot that the urban muggers and rapists all were cowering indoors in front of the television, praying for an afternoon movie about the Klondike and spit cracking like a shot between lip and ground.

I got an egg and a skillet and went out to the sidewalk.

There is no walk on my side of the street, so I went across to my neighbor's side and sat down on the pavement and melted the grease in the skillet and broke the egg into it.

A friend from several houses down came past in her car. She stopped and got out.

"What are you doing?" she asked.

"Frying an egg on the sidewalk," I told her.

"Well," she said, "it's hot enough."

"Maybe it is and maybe it isn't. That's what I'm trying to find out."

"Did you preheat your skillet?" she asked.

"I didn't think of that. But it's an aluminum skillet. Aluminum is a good conductor."

"You should have preheated your skillet."

Look, I wanted to say, I didn't ask for a lot of gratuitous advice. This is my egg. You want to do it some other way, get your own egg. There's sidewalk enough for both of us.

But I didn't say that. She is a friend, so I bit my lip. And together — me sitting on the pavement, her standing, her car left parked in the middle of the street — we watched the egg.

"You're throwing a shadow," I told her. "You'll attract dogs and cats and birds and caterpillars."

"Huh?" she said. And moved a little to the side.

The neighbor whose sidewalk I was cooking on came home unexpectedly in midafternoon from his place of business. He stopped in the drive and came over where we were.

"What the devil are you doing?" he said.

"Frying an egg."

It was perfectly obvious what I was doing. There was the skillet, the egg, the spatula poised expectantly in my hand.

"That's what I thought," he said. He is, I believe, a man of a literal turn. "Going anywhere this summer?" he asked. "Taking any little trips?" Maybe he was of the opinion that I needed to get away for a while.

"I've been up in Michigan," he said. "It's been hot there, too." Then he looked at the skillet with the egg in it. "But not this hot." And he got back in his car and drove away again, not wanting to be associated with the activity on his sidewalk.

The friend from down the block got in her car, too.

"I still say you should have preheated your skillet," she said.

And I was alone then with my egg, which remained in

its initial condition — the yolk floating in a puddle of transparent goo. After more than an hour there still was no change. It would not cook.

But such is the force of hyperbole that we all believed it might.

"You'll never guess what I saw today," the friend probably reported later. "I saw old so-and-so up the block frying an egg on the sidewalk."

Truth be damned. The image still has power. The legend lives.

THE OUTLET MALL

Like those sylvan lakes that pool among the dunes and dry escarpments of the Sahara, the mirage of a shopping center rose shimmering out of the unpeopled vastness of the High Plains.

I choked back a scream. *It couldn't be!* reason said. It was, though.

An Outlet Mall.

Traffic was slowing and veering off the interstate in an unbroken stream, the cars bearing toward a vast parking lot and discharging human persons, mostly of the female gender, all shiny-eyed as Imelda Marcos in a shoe store.

"Build it," a voice had told some merchant king, *"and they will come."*

So there amid the rolling pastures and fields of irrigated sorghum, with no town visible in any direction, the abomination stood — an unseemly wart on the silken breast of the land. And the people came. At one side, the bulldozers were still at work, leveling more acres so the beachhead of commerce could be enlarged.

I don't know what it is about such places that provokes the feeding frenzy. The magic must be in the word *outlet*. Or maybe it is the setting, out there at the edge of nowhere, where the hot winds blowing up from Sonora and whining at the building corners hint at awful regions of abandonment where credit cards are not accepted.

Whatever the explanation, it was clear that monstrosity astride the prairie had inspired in lots of people a powerful rage to buy. To be absolutely fair about it, some of the male travelers were buying, too. But most, like me, looked hopelessly around for some shady place, or leaned against their car fenders and sadly smoked.

Time passed. Much time.

Ahead — unimaginably far away in this wasted interlude — the mountains waited. There the air would be fresh, the trails steep, the odor of pine needles sharp and clean.

Maybe we would get there sometime and maybe not. The ladies of my life had been swallowed up in the Outlet Mall and I was powerless to call them back. What if the mountains were never in their plan at all? What if we'd come 300 miles just to buy a glass dish for microwaving broccoli?

Heat rose in visible waves from the asphalt parking lot. Straight overhead, in the deep of the cloudless sky, a gang of buzzards circled, riding the thermals that reflected from the roofs of the cars. I counted them, and there were 17 buzzards. Even far up as they were, you could see how their heads bent down, eyes fixed on the Outlet Mall.

It got me nervous, and I made a turn of the parking lot on foot to see if there might be something or someone dead between the rows of cars. No tragedies were to be found, beyond the larger tragedy of the place itself.

I came back, then, and sat inside the car where I wouldn't have to see the nasty birds turning, turning overhead.

"*Start it,*" I heard a voice say.

At first I didn't know where the voice was coming from. Or what it meant. Then the car keys were in my hand, without my quite knowing how they got there. Then the keys were in the ignition.

"*Start it,*" said the voice. "*Start it . . . and maybe they will come.*"

The next thing I remember the car was headed westward on the interstate, straight into the swollen brilliance of the late sun, and my ladies were in the car with me.

When I looked in the rearview mirror, the mirage, if that's what it was, had sunk below the horizon. And the road to higher country lay clear ahead.

SLOWING TIME

The mornings were rainy, the afternoons clear and fresh, the nights cool. In the deep of summer, days like those are gifts.

Best of all, there was no melancholy.

There have been occasions in these last years, all alone in the cabin at the edge of the woods, when the shadows of people and times past have been too many. But this was one of those rare chances for both daughters to come with me, so the place was fine.

The jigsaw puzzle we'd assembled on a cold evening last winter still was on the table. We broke it back into its 1,000 pieces to be saved for another time. The pond gave up its fish. Afterward, we burned some chicken haunches on the grill, turning them by flashlight. In the meadow just north of the cabin woods, coyotes set up a racket of yipping and giggling in the dark.

We talked a while. Then slept. And in the morning made a project of cleaning out and rearranging our fishing tackle boxes — remembering, as one always does, the fish that came to certain lures, and where that water was, and how the curve of the reed bed lay against the shore, and if the day was blistering or chill.

It's a humble place, that little retreat of ours — the cabin small and rude, the beds miserable, the plumbing delicate and undependable. The pictures on the walls contain good moments, though. The faces in them are ones we've cared the most about. The lane that bends from the porch down through the oak forest to the little lake has been traveled on foot so many times, beginning when I was hardly more than a boy, that I can follow it unerringly even in the dark of the moon.

The last morning we fished a creek — got worm slime on our hands, saw several great blue herons rising from the shallows, got chigger bites and ticks, caught poison ivy, dug wildflowers to put in the garden at home, then drove the highway back.

I'm surprised to find how little there is to tell, and yet these primitive amusements so filled two days and part of a third that it seemed we'd been weeks and a great distance away.

As life progresses, time gets to be of great concern. Weeks and months pass unremarked, becoming years, the years resolving into sudden decades. Much human ingenuity is devoted to trying to halt the rush.

Some say work's the answer, but I disagree. Work can surely make a day seem endless. It does nothing to slow the larger clock. Others put their faith in running shoes and dietary fiber, thinking those will enable them to cheat mortality a bit.

Personally, I favor sloth and idleness — attributes which command their proper respect in that stretch of woodland to which we from time to time repair. If ever I'm too conscious of the ring of time closing, that's where I mean to go.

I'll unplug the radio, disconnect the phone, give the typewriter to anyone who'll have it, devote myself to singing with the spring toads, baying with the hounds in fall, and listening to the woodbox mice in winter while I assemble the jigsaw puzzle yet again.

WATCH YOUR MOUTH, MISTER

Inspectors from a consumer watchdog group dropped in recently to see how government guidelines were being followed at a certain country cafe where folks of my rural neighborhood regularly assemble.

It was the breakfast hour, and the place was wall-to-wall with farmers in coveralls and hunters in orange jackets, all calling out for their morning ration of grease.

You could spot the inspectors right away by their suits and ties and the clipboards they were carrying. The waitress, Bobbie Sue, put their plates in front of them.

"Excuse me, young lady," one of them said to her. "Could you tell me at what temperature these eggs were cooked?"

"Over easy," she told him. "Like you asked."

"No," he said. "I mean the actual cooking temperature."

Mornings there get pretty busy, and Bobbie Sue didn't have a lot of time for foolishness.

"Hey, Thelma," she bawled back in the general direction of the kitchen, where the cook was setting new orders up in the window.

"Fella out here got a question."

Every head in the place turned to look at the table of suits.

"Wants to know how hot is his eggs."

A titter passed through the crowd.

"Never mind," the man said. "I'll see for myself."

He took a small black case from his pocket, got out a thermometer and thrust the end of it into the liquid yolk of one of his eggs-over-easy. Then he wrote something down on his clipboard.

"That just won't do," he said, tapping the paper with his finger. "And I see where the lunch special is fried chicken. I'm very concerned about that."

"What's he sayin' now?" the cook, Thelma, called from the kitchen.

"He's worried about your chicken."

The cook replied with a word that can't be printed here, and the men in coveralls and orange jackets all laughed out loud.

"You tell him I been fryin' chicken longer'n he's been alive," she cried out indignantly. "And there hasn't been no complaints yet."

"That's right," several of the regulars said.

"You bet! Best damned chicken anyplace around."

The mood in the place was beginning to tense up.

"One more thing," the inspector said to Bobbie Sue. "When were you last tested for communicable diseases?"

"Say what?"

"If you wouldn't mind, I'd like to see your current health certificate."

"Lordy!" said the waitress, and she threw up her hands in hopelessness. "Now he's saying maybe I got something nasty."

That was the last straw. Bobbie Sue was a great favorite there in the place. A general grumble was heard, and some of the other patrons, several of them rather large, started to get up from their chairs.

"Never mind," said the inspector. "Just let us have our check."

Bobbie Sue took their money at the register, smiling as if nothing at all out of the way had ever happened.

"Have a nice day," she said. "And remember us the next time you're through here."

Friendliness like that keeps folks coming back.

ANGEL PIE HAS A TICK

The common wood tick (also called the hard tick, the dog tick and, less often, *Dermacentor variabilis*) is not an elegant creature. But he is durable. You will have to give him that.

Each spring for well over a century the settlers of our southern forest have been setting the woodlands afire in persistent faith that it will kill the ticks. The wildfires rage. Houses burn. Barns burn, with machinery in them. Horses go mad. Valuable timber stands are scarred and destroyed. Wildlife is driven out.

But spend several hours marching on foot across the still-smoking wasteland of gray ash and you will come back clung over by ticks.

In the stretch of hills I know best, the stream courses and early wagon roads are dotted with the stone footings of vanished dwellings. Some of those homesteads, it may safely be supposed, were consumed by fires set to kill the ticks. Habitation has thinned. And still there are ticks — in multiples of human numbers.

I have read that the tick has been known to live three years without food or drink. I take my hat off not only to the tick but to whichever scientist it was whose patience and constant observation we have to thank for that amazing piece of information.

Can you imagine the resourcefulness, the sheer *chutzpah*, it would take to secure a federal grant to spend three years watching a tick do nothing?

Perhaps more amazing even than his ability to withstand hunger and thirst is the reaction this insignificant creature is able to arouse in soft-skinned city people meeting him for the first time. Upon discovering that the thing is on them, and, worse, that it is *attached to them*, the fact of this misfortune is made known in whispers.

The afflicted count it no consolation that this tick — their tick — may have waited three years for a drink. A transport of shame and revulsion overcomes them. They speak of their condition as one might discuss a social disease.

Husbands and wives, mothers and children, closely related adults of the same gender, withdraw into the next room and lock the door. There is a long, speculative silence. Presently the door is unlocked and an emissary is dispatched.

Angel Pie has a tick.

This vouchsafed in a low voice, eyes averted, the face of the bearer of the news flushed with humiliation.

"Has she? Well, that's good. Ticks only go for warm-blooded animals, so it must mean that Angel Pie is hot-blooded."

I'm serious. She has a tick. It's a small one.

"Yes. They all start small."

What should I do? She's in a state.

"Pull it off."

The emissary is recalled for consultation. Then emerges again.

She says she can't pull it off.

"All right." Taking a step toward the closed door. "I'll do it for her."

No! Wait a minute!

Invariably, then, the tick is gotten off unaided.

Covering a tick with petroleum jelly is rumored to cause it to release its grip. A daub of nail polish is said also to be effective — the more expensive polishes, naturally, producing a superior result. Some advise holding a lighted match near the parasite, although, depending on location, the consequence of that can be tragic for the host.

Country people, after a century of failed burning, have no faith in these measures. And I have spent enough time among them to adopt their casual attitude, which is that ticks, like morel mushrooms and wildflowers in bloom, are simply part of the natural order of the season.

Some come off in the bath. Some you have to pull off. Most of the others, after enough time has passed and they have achieved sufficient size, sooner or later come out in the comb.

You would be surprised how the explanation of this reduces the congestion of weekend visitors at our cabin at the edge of the woods.

A WILD THING PASSING

Self-contained and businesslike as a constable on his rounds, a red fox trotted across our yard the other evening. By luck, I was looking down from the upstairs window at just that moment and saw him pass.

There long have been foxes denning along the creek beside the golf course several blocks away. And another family of them, bringing off their litters of kits on a street where a friend lives.

But those are rock-ledged and foliaged places. Ours is just a regular city block, with houses in a row and mown yards adjoining. We've had opossums and raccoons in the storm sewers, and chipmunks in a crevice under the step, and rabbits in the flower garden. Never a fox, though — not in the nearly 30 years we've had the house.

First I saw a movement down through the screening leaves of the crab apple tree. Rabbit, my mind computed, because it was that hour, just before sundown, when our two regulars come out to graze.

Then he passed from under the tree and into clear view. *No, a dog, my mind corrected itself. Handsome, reddish dog — same color as the hair of a girl I used to know. But something undoglike about that bushy tail, flowing straight behind, tipped with black. Dog with a tail just like a fox. A foxish dog. No! Wait! That's no dog at all!*

Absolutely unexpected meetings with Nature can addle you that way.

I called for my wife, and we rushed downstairs together

to see if we could spy him again. But he'd trotted on out of sight. He could have been one of those from the creek by the golf course, we decided, because that was the general direction he was heading. Maybe, in this season of young ones to feed, they'd cleaned out all the mice and rabbits in their usual territory and had found it necessary to expand their range.

Then we thought about our own rabbits, which we like having around to speak to when we go out at daylight to pick up the paper or come in from somewhere late at night.

"Do you suppose he got them?" I wondered aloud. I hadn't noticed him carrying anything when he passed, but you never know. No rabbits were seen that night, or again the next morning. I suspected the worst.

But then, the more I thought about it, I began to be reconciled to taking Nature as she comes, in all her sweetness and ferocity. If you get one, you get both. And after everything that's been done to tame the land to man's service, we're lucky to have anything wild still sharing our beaten space.

I underestimated rabbits, though. The next evening, our same two were back, chewing grass and flower leaves as if they hadn't a worry in the world.

They know that the cats watching them from inside our screened windows are not allowed to roam. They know the bird dog asleep in his house is slow afoot. They know the tunnels through the flowers and the spaces under the board fence where only a rabbit can fit.

And when the fox comes only once in 30 years, there's time enough to plan.

IF AUTUMN WERE A GIRL

There's a chill in the mornings now. The light comes later. The shadows are sharper. Suddenly as a drawn breath, we've made the turning toward that season of things remembered and other things expected.

The important weight of school books newly bought. Pencils whose erasers haven't yet been worn to nubs. New friends. Noisy afternoons on a practice field. Leave-takings — first to school in another town, and after that to barracks life.

Always, it seemed, this moment of the year's change was a time of fresh beginnings.

The other morning I rose at an early hour, in darkness, and drove to the place of country friends. There was no sign of stirring at the house, so I left the car and walked along a field's edge to a prominence from which there was a grand view of the land falling away in every direction.

The dawn came on, revealing that piece of the world in splendid clarity — the dark of woods, the fine pattern of alternating pastures and uncut crop fields. Blackbirds were fluttering above it all in immense numbers. The air was full of their chittering. It was the only sound.

Then, wet to knees from the dew, I went back to the house and sat a happy hour over coffee with those friends at their table. We looked ahead, made plans together. And I left there renewed, as I always do.

Another morning I took the bird dog pups for exercise on a tract of public land in a different direction. It's a grand place of meadows and standing crops and shining lakes.

The pups are soft from their indolence of summer, but who am I to speak of softness? That morning, though, we covered miles without tiring. The two dog-brothers explored every patch of thicket and woods, coursed happily over open fields, swam when it pleased them, and even pointed a startled box tortoise.

The greenery's still too lush for much serious work. The foliage will need to be burned by a hard freeze before the scent of the hidden bird can come to them strong and clear. Our outings now are just to harden us up a bit for the season ahead.

But all the rituals of early rising, the car ride, the freedom of that unfenced ground, and afterward the picking out of seeds tangled in their fur — everything reminds them, and me, of the glory days ahead.

Always, on these outings in the turning of the year, I am thinking at once of times and people gone and of new friends found and new adventures waiting. The memories are more powerful now than ever, and the expectations keener.

It's that mix of eagerness and wistfulness you feel when, as you hurry toward some celebration, you remember others that were no less fine. It is, in fact, the mingled sweetness and regret of all our lives.

If autumn were a girl, I'd propose to her. If autumn were a wine, I'd settle for no other. And if autumn were a place, I would hope to live there always.

I CAN'T MANAGE THE UNIVERSE

The planet tilts a fraction in its spinning, and suddenly the midday brilliance of our star is bearable, the nights are fresh for sleeping and the hour of getting up is blue again.

Yesterday, some creature began a hole alongside our house foundation, throwing up a tailing of mealy dirt at the entrance of its burrow. Today, I saw the proprietor of that hole dart across the driveway and vanish in a patch of undergrowth. A chipmunk was who he was — autumn fat, but caught up in the season's fury of preparation.

I meant to fill his excavation — scoop the earth back in, tamp it firm and maybe put a rock atop the place for good measure. He might have a house to make, but I have one to guard. I actually went so far as to fetch the shovel. But then I measured the product of all that digging against the size of the digger, and found that, in the end, I couldn't do it. Next spring, maybe, but not now, not in the year's changing. The porous basement wall won't be fatally hurt by one more seep. Not the way that things alive can be hurt by bad luck or error in this season.

Managing the universe would be an awful responsibility to have to bear — deciding which things would bite and which be bitten, which ones would spin webs and which be caught in them, which ones would sleep a winter safely through and which perish with the frost. Complicated judgments, those, and very final. And the accident of belonging to the race of things that hammers iron and makes shovels may not entitle one to meddle in the process.

That was my line of reasoning, anyway, about the chipmunk and his hole. From his perspective I may loom fairly omnipotent. But I know better. Like him, I'm just another creature bearing on toward the solstice, with only so much margin for error, only so much credit to spend. And from this recognition flows a certain passivity, a flabbiness of will that worsens year by year.

As in the matter of the kitten that, a fortnight ago, presented itself a slight and large-eyed wanderer at our door. Yes, *another* one. Harden your hearts, I commanded. But the visitor was let in. All right, then, we'll *give it away.* Then the heat of summer broke. A cool wind sent leaves spinning down. The cat, never once imagining the world might have no place for it, found the food dish, the softest chair cushion, the place on the window sill where the late sun falls. Made homage to the older cats and was accepted. Reached a friendly understanding with the dogs. And finally, in the dark of one morning, like the others before it, was discovered beside us in the bed.

He's one of us now. Tardily, some folks have said they'd like to have him. But nothing could persuade us to give him up. He's a cat beyond price. Just as that chipmunk is my chipmunk, and I'll have no stranger or neighbor messing with his hole.

Children and parents . . . wives and hunting dogs . . . chipmunks and deed-holders of wet foundations — where, in any of that, is there an easy fit? Into the dark of the year we go together, and I take no responsibility. Whatever flung us together will have to sort us out.

III

THE SPLENDID ARCHITECT

The autumn spider is at work in an untended space beside the house.

I once had the idea to make a raised garden there — built up a wall of railroad ties and hauled in a quantity of earth and mulch. But in a season the weeds defeated me. The place is abandoned now to a tangle of euonymus and tree sprouts.

That corner is just outside the window of my wife's flower room, which also is where I work. The other morning, coming to water her plants, she stopped in the doorway and cried out in delight: "Oh, look at it!"

"At what?"

"That wonderful spider web. See it? Just there between the window and the fence."

The angle of the early sun struck it in a way that caused each individual strand and the fabulous larger geometry to stand out with perfect clarity.

In all, the web covered an area nearly as great as a wash tub, all of it suspended from a master cable strung horizontally between a branch of the climbing euonymus and the tip of a head-high mulberry sprout.

The author of that masterpiece, a fat-bodied garden spider, could be seen moving industriously about, inserting more cross-members, reinforcing and perfecting her construction.

For several days after that I remembered to notice her advancing work. I never saw even one blundering moth entangled in the web, but utility was not its point. When a little breeze stirred the foliage to which it was anchored, the whole splendid edifice trembled and shone like a silver net shaken.

Then came a night of harder winds. And the next morning only wreckage was left. The upper cable was broken. The rest hung in tatters, and the spider herself was nowhere to be seen. I wondered where she had gone. And whether, if she had begun another silver net like that one, she had been a little choosier about what she anchored it to.

Then, today, I saw she had been at work again.

Lower down, protected amid the thicker foliage, were new webs. Five of them — small ones, no bigger than your hand — but tucked cleverly away among the branches to surprise any winged or creeping thing that strayed that way.

Of course, there's no proving the same spider built them, but that was her general territory and it seems reasonable to think she did.

I like to believe that first soaring masterpiece was her magnum opus, erected for the pure glory of doing it, and to show what a miraculous tapestry the imagination can weave.

These later ones, clearly, are a commoner sort of work, thrown up out of the same necessity that drives us all — to put a beetle or two on the table.

But the autumn's short, and need is long. And even an artist has to eat.

AYATOLLAH OF THE LEAVES

Ours is an amiable block — tree-shaded and outwardly quite serene, as neighborly a street as you would hope to find. We cry hearty greetings when carrying out our plastic bags on trash collection day and make complimentary remarks about the greenness of one another's lawns and are careful to keep garage doors closed when not in use.

The observance of these small but important protocols enables us to feel warmth and comradeship and a certain sense of shared purpose.

In recent autumns, though, an ugly current of tension has arisen. And that is saddening, the more so because of knowing that I am the cause of it — or, rather, my leaves are. My attitude toward leaves is flagrantly casual, even irresponsible. And this is seen by some as symptomatic of a dangerous and more general indiscipline of mind and habit and moral posture. It was not always so.

The previous owner of my house left behind a large, wheeled machine which, when pushed across the lawn, snatched up the leaves with its wire fingers and deposited them in a catcher behind. We took occupancy in early November and I spent much of the next two months attached to the handle of that machine.

The sun never set on a fallen leaf. The lawn was routinely swept before guests. And I was alert to every breeze. If a vagrant leaf spun down, I would rush outside with a little cry of shame and pluck it up by hand. The neighbors must have observed all this with pleasure and admiration. For my zeal exceeded even their own.

Then winter bore down. And in the retrospect of a different season, it came to me that perhaps leaf-gathering was not, after all, a career worthy of the devotion of a life. In that moment of apostasy, the seeds of the present ill will were sown.

Part of the fault is Nature's.

Leaves do not come down all at once. The diseased elms drop theirs first, followed in leisurely turn by the ash, the maples and — much later — the pin oak. Now I perfectly understand that all this leaf-litter must eventually be collected and disposed of. Otherwise the clock of the year could not turn. There would be no lawns. And without lawns there would be no civility.

But it also seems reasonable to let all the leaves fall before the task of gathering begins. Otherwise it is an enterprise as endless as cleaning the Augean stables with a dinner fork.

The logic is flawless. But there comes into play a second problem, the wind, which in autumn tends to be gusting and capricious.

The man next door owns an elaborate, motor-driven apparatus for shredding leaves and putting them automatically into bags. But his spirit is broken. The machine stays in his garage. He now only bothers to rake the half of his yard that is farthest from mine, and he goes about that desultorily. At other times of the year he is most cordial, but between the first frost and the first snowfall he hardly speaks.

Other neighbors across the street recently moved away.

That man, too, kept an immaculate lawn. He was kindly and soft-spoken, not inclined to stir an argument. But when my leaves swirled up to ride the wind his way, I could detect in his manner something of heartbreak and mute reproach. And I will always wonder if that was part of his reason for going.

New people are in that house now. The other evening I heard a lawnmower running and shouts of industry, and saw that they were out bagging leaves. After dark. By porch light and flashlight. Their earnestness is as impressive as mine was that first autumn on the street. I am sorry to think of the discouragements ahead for them. For, even as they labored, my million or so troops were rustling and scuttering impatiently at the curb, waiting to be loosed.

And it occurred to me then that, in my neighbors' view, I must be a sort of Ayatollah of the Leaves. A brooding figure of unreason and dark intent. A man whose understanding of the world and of decent behavior is not their own. The unleasher of chaos — of humorless and desecrating multitudes beyond even my own control.

And until the first deep snow comes to still my hordes and break my power, they and their tidy lawns will remain my hostages.

MORNING BECOMES ELECTRIC

*S*urprise, says the poet, *is the cinnamon in the bun, the brandy in the coffee, the sugar on the pudding of life.*

Actually, I can find no record of any poet having written exactly that. But since poets have said almost everything imaginable, surely somewhere, sometime, one must have.

The company that makes the weekly trash collection on our block knows, as the poet does, that surprise is beneficial, and has gone to the trouble of arranging its schedule in a way that will avoid monotony and keep us emotionally alive.

Sometimes the truck comes before we have awakened in the morning, with our plastic bags still in the garage, affording us the small adventure of cohabiting a second week with a rich mix of junk mail, chicken bones and mellowing cantaloupe rinds.

Sometimes the pickup is deferred until late evening out of consideration for the dogs which, prospecting freely along the block, are able in a leisurely way to sort through the contents of the sacks for merchandise of possible latent use.

The beauty is that there is no pattern to it. No predictability. Which gives to trash collection day an element of fine suspense.

The other morning, for example, just on the edge of sleep — after the clock radio had begun its muted crooning, but before the opening of eyes — a premonitory rumble was heard from the lower end of the street. It was the sound of the compactor ingesting its first half-dozen bags.

The response was galvanic. All along the block doors were flung open and semi-clad householders leapt out with expressions of blind panic, dragging sacks of gin bottles and limp lime twists and putrefied hors d'oeuvres.

Such moments have a social usefulness. One gets to see what one's neighbors wear to sleep in. Modesty is subordinate to terror. Substantial citizens can be observed running barefoot up the street after the driver, as if the fellow played a magic flute. The event affords, for us in the provinces, the same kind of necessary stimulation that residents of the more sophisticated Eastern cities must find in brownouts, muggings and occasional derailments of commuter trains.

Probably it would be easier, from the trash collector's viewpoint, to travel his route according to a fixed schedule, each week the same. Easier, yes — but dull. His days and ours would lapse into flat routine. So, quite unselfishly, he takes pains to keep alive the element of surprise.

High up behind the windshield of his truck, his face is impassive. But as the doors open and we burst into the blue morning like fighter pilots running to our planes, he must feel rewarded by a quiet pride at the part he has played in unleashing so vigorous a spectacle.

Afterward we all stand panting at the curb and watch the truck pass on.

Sleep is gone out of us. One moment we were languishing abed. The next moment we are at full stride and fever pitch. Our morning has begun with intensity — and begun, moreover, with a shining victory.

Only the dogs are disappointed.

THE SEASON'S WITCHING HOUR

The upper bedroom, at the hour for sleeping, was as breathless on that recent night as on all the ones before it. Bedclothes crinkled and clung.

From somewhere up the block a dog's irritable barking was borne on the heavy air. On the branch outside the window, a tracing of dry summer leaves hung still as something darkly painted against the sky.

The weather forecast told of a front approaching from the north. But surely it must be very far away. For the wind that began to stir in the last moment before dreaming was only another dry exhalation of an unkind season endlessly prolonged.

Later, though, a fitful waker found a change. Still stifling the room was. But something had silenced the creaking insects, had even smitten mute the yipping dog. A sense of expectation was afoot in that strange hour.

The night was full of prophecy — a prophecy not of new things but half-recollected old ones, scuttering wind-driven along the shadow-ways of half a hundred years. And sleep would not come now, that much was sure.

The waker sat on the bed's edge, bent sideways to the window, nose into the wind like a wolf's, taking in the messages, trying to remember what it was that he remembered.

How suddenly, then, it happened.

In a single instant the mutter in the trees became a thrashing. Another instant and the hotness was gone —

the smell of burnt grass having given way to the keener smells of wet prairie and, beyond that, great reaching forest and of a still farther place of that wind's rising out of the hoarfrost and the endless ice.

The cold rain, riding horizontal on the blast, drove through the open window. The cat leapt down with a growl from his summer place on the sill.

The wind passed, and the street outside shone wetly in the light. The stifle of the room was gone — swept away more quickly and more surely than is possible by any machine. A sheet had to be drawn up, and after that a blanket.

The half-memories came finally clear: of colored leaf-showers in long-ago parks, of burning leaf-piles glowing white-orange at their heart, of quick departings, of stalk bent and thistle blown, of winged travelers crying down their loneliness from the mapless dark.

All of this happening in the unbelievably shortest of time — less time than it takes to write it or even to read it.

With terrible carelessness our seasons are apt to pass. But unlike the autumns of all those earlier years, this one had been witnessed at the exact moment of its turning. And then, the pillow cool, there was nothing else to wait awake for.

LIFE ON THE EDGE

"Let's have a fire in the fireplace," I said to my wife.

"I suppose we could," she replied. "But the house really isn't that cold."

"Believe me, it soon will be."

"How do you know that?" she said.

"I know it because the furnace isn't working."

We have this conversation every year, as the leaves and the weather start to turn.

The furnace is original equipment, installed when the house was built. Made to burn coal, it has been twice converted, first to oil and then to gas. The boiler is the size, roughly, of a 1950 Packard, constructed of cast iron, and weighs 145,406 pounds. The man who built the house never imagined any reason why the furnace would need to be removed. It is impossible to see any way it *could* be removed, unless by using explosives to demolish the east wall of the dining room and basement and winching the leviathan up and out through the hole.

So we are joined for the duration, the furnace and I. Each fall it refuses to fire. I mention this regrettable situation to my wife, and as soon as the household budget allows — usually before hypothermia has dulled our wits and numbed our fingers through the mittens — I ring up the specialist to come have a look.

He may be the only living craftsman still familiar with heating units of such great antiquity, and he approaches the thing with the same delicacy and profound respect archaeologists displayed in their handling of artifacts from the tomb of King Tut.

At least twice, the boiler has sprung leaks and then, mysteriously, has healed itself. Sometimes the ailment is major. This time it was trifling — a single clogged pipe. As soon as it was unstopped, the burner fired.

"We'll let it build up a head of steam," he said. "Then we'll know if there are any other problems."

Heating 145,406 pounds of cast iron to the point where it will vaporize water takes time. Much time. The furnace specialist is a fine conversationalist, and we have opportunity to catch up on one another's families, solve most of society's problems and discuss a wide range of foreign policy issues.

"You're living on the edge," he said, as he put his tools back in their case.

His words did not alarm me. It's how I am used to living. I am extremely comfortable on the edge.

"If it makes it through this winter," he said, "I think you'll be faced with a decision in the spring."

He has been telling me that for years. Each time, after he has coaxed and massaged it a bit, the furnace has rumbled to life and warmed us the winter through. This time, though, he sounded like he might really mean it.

"What did he say?" my wife asked after he'd left.

"He said he'd bill us for the work."

"No, I mean about the furnace."

"The usual. He said we're doomed."

"But I hear it running down there."

"Yes, it's heating."

"And the cats are on the radiators," she said. "It's a

good sign."

Then the weather turned fair again, and the crisis passed from mind.

The furnace specialist still is in his prime, and iron is durable. It's just possible, as the song in *archy and mehitabel* goes, that "there's a dance in the old dame yet."

THE GIFT OF PLENTY

The festive spirit has claimed our house. The floors are polished. The rugs and upholstery have been cleansed of the malfeasances of dogs and cats. Friends will be joining us at the holiday table, and I have risen in darkness to stuff and bake the Thanksgiving opossum.

Probably there will be snide comments. Our friends are not the kind of people who hide their ill will under a bushel.

"What's that thing on the platter?"

"It's the Thanksgiving possum," I will reply evenly, as I carve. "Light meat or dark?"

A mutter of outrage will pass among them.

"Is this some kind of joke? We're supposed to get turkey. It's a national tradition."

"Since when?"

"Since the Pilgrims. The Indians brought the Pilgrims a turkey."

"Listen," I will tell them, "the Pilgrims were a bunch of losers, down on their luck. Winter was coming on and they were hungry. Then the Indians showed up with some food."

"With a turkey."

"OK, so it was a turkey. But it could have been any-thing. Some days the Indians had buffalo tongue. Other times it was porcupine or bear meat. That day they just happened to have a turkey. *Big deal!*"

"Are you implying that Turkey Day is an empty tradi-tion?"

"I am only saying that if the Indians had come with a possum, the Pilgrims — who were a sorry, ragtag outfit — would have been mighty glad to get it. They would have smacked their lips and declared that henceforth, forever, the last Thursday in November would be known as Possum Day. People would stand in line at the supermarket to get their Butterball possums."

"You got that thing at a store?"

"No, it was a gift."

"From an Indian?"

"A gift of luck. I got it yesterday afternoon on Bannis-ter Road with my right front tire, a glancing blow. It was hardly even bruised."

The guests will sit with their clenched fists on the table beside their plates, knives and forks sticking straight up from their fists. They will make no effort to hide their dis-appointment.

"The last time we came for Thanksgiving you had a turkey."

"That was the last time. Before they went off half-cocked to the New World to starve as Pilgrims, the Pilgrims sat around their cozy fireplaces in London and ate plum pudding. Things change. Now I am a man in the twilight of his powers, made bankrupt by putting two daughters through college at once, and I am a ragtag Pilgrim who takes what he is given. If a turkey had crossed the road yesterday, we would have had turkey. What I was given, however, was a possum. We will eat it together in fellowship and gratitude."

"Not me!"

"Me either!"

The drumming of the handles of their knives and forks on the table will make an awful racket.

"For the blessings of this day," my daughters will intone reverently. "And for the blessings of financial aid and federal student loans that may one day be repaid . . ."

Shamed to silence, our guests will stare at the main course.

"Here we are, all together once more!" I will sing out heartily. "The harvest is in. The frost is on the pumpkin and the corn is in the shock."

They will look back at me with gray, flat faces.

"So speak up now," I will tell them again, "light meat or dark?"

IN THE EYE OF A HAWK

It is the season of the hawks.

The sky pales. Frost burns the prairie grasses, and the north wind coming keen-edged across the vastness of the Flint Hills sets seed pods rattling dryly on leafless stalks.

The surplus of the greener time has been drawn down, the land laid bare. All is seen now as if in a photograph of incredible sharpness, but drained of tone. And above that the hawks turn or frown down motionless from their post-top perches.

Most of us have never looked near at hand into a hawk's eye. Some of us might not care to. But the fierceness of that stare can be imagined. Certainly the small furred things that creep among the grasses can imagine it — though they have never seen it either and, if they do, will see it only once.

Under such a sky, on such a day, with feathered hunters wheeling on the wind, we climb a pitch of prairie barrens and drop down into a fold where trees mark the course of a winding seep, then climb again. I am hiking with two friends: one of them met not many days ago, the other a longer friend who has gone on foot through a part of these hills before, and who has a fair acquaintance with the plants that contrive to prosper in the grassy sea, making their rush of bloom in spring and then browning in this time of year, but durably surviving.

His knowledge of these things richens the day.

Together we top another rise and look far down a dry

wash to where a pond glitters, small as a silver coin, and beyond that to the smaller specks of cattle standing dark against the tan of sod.

Except for the hawks, the cattle specks and us, there seems no other life in that immensity until we descend finally to the pond, where frogs are splashing. We find there the medallion-sized shell of a turtle that died without quite getting to the water, and the open shells of small freshwater clams stranded by summer's drought.

Something brown scuttles in the grass at our feet. A vole, we guess it to be. Then a prairie chicken takes wing nearby and sails over the lip of the hillside. These are the things we are able to see, on a day when the spareness of autumn has laid the country open to our eye.

What then must the hawks see, with their cold and infinitely finer vision? Above us they hang upon the wind in their astonishing numbers. No doubt they see the whole pattern of the land, and so are never lost, as we are lost. They see the larger objects — three figures walking down a slope and up another and down again, bound on some errand about which hawks are indifferent.

But their purpose is more discriminate.

Patiently they turn — for long minutes, for effortless hours. But in an instant the wings fold back. And, cowering among the dead stems, some creature hears the rush of wind and looks a first-last time into hunger's yellow eye.

Hawks rule here, and this is their season. But by the pure luck of being an awkward size for a meal, we are able to gain the valley and find the car.

THE HIRED GUN

The excitement stirred by the impending arrival of Deadline Duffenback, big time journalist from The East, has been unkindly punctured. Duffenback isn't coming. He's staying put.

We who ply our trade here in the provinces get fairly wrought up over word of a hired gun riding in from one of the flashier places. As people around the newsroom have been saying lately, "If Duffenback's coming, can Pulitzer be far behind?"

As often as not, though, there's only disappointment in it.

Sometimes these prize catches are in and gone again before anyone learns their names. One of them, I'm told, started traveling west by car. And as the stillness of the barbarian interior closed around him, his heart sickened and his courage failed. He resigned after two days among us.

Another, as I recall, took the better part of half a year to find his way here. Periodic situation reports pinned to the bulletin board told of his erratic progress. Maps with dotted lines, circulated among the staff, traced his slow advance.

By the time he actually got here, some of the people he was supposed to lead had aged and retired, a couple had died, and quite a few others had gotten discouraged, torn up their press cards and fallen on good times and useful work. He, too, was a short-timer.

Deadline Duffenback, however, has set a new record. He has taken the job, and quit it, without ever leaving New York.

Maybe he was indispensable there. Or maybe the imminence of his leaving made him *seem* indispensable. Is it mean-spirited to think he may accidentally have let drop some veiled hint of his plan to bolt to the hinterlands?

"It's a savage place Out There," his employers would have told Duffenback. To them, our part of the country doesn't have place names. It's all just *Out There.*

"But I've already taken the job."

"So?"

"Notices of my coming have been posted. A storm of excitement has risen. Their cup runneth over. They are waiting to pipe me on board."

"You're mixing your metaphors, Deadline. It's one of the things we've never liked about you. But you're a promising kid. We'd hate for you to go Out There and just disappear in the wilderness. How can we change your mind?"

"I'll have to think about it."

"How long do you need?"

"That was plenty of time."

"So what will it take to keep you."

"Money will do it. A few thou, and a company car."

So, in the end, the deal with Deadline Duffenback fell through. The notice about his coming was taken down from the bulletin board, and a new one had to be put up, saying he wasn't coming after all and we'd have to go it alone. I can tell you, people have been pretty down-at-the-mouth and blue around here in recent days.

About Deadline's actual talents as a journalist we don't know much. But we'd bet anything he plays a mean game of poker.

WHERE GOURMETS MEET

There never has been a report of anyone actually dying from the food in the employee lunch room. But then, it is a large company with a lot of workers, and things have been known to go on here that weren't learned about for years.

I look around from time to time and wonder where so many of the old faces have gone. It is entirely possible that some of them slumped over their plates at the tables upstairs and were quietly dragged off and stacked up somewhere — under the steam counter, perhaps — to await disposition by the next in the succession of vendors.

The menu, although plain, is not without variety. There is the Brown Stuff, the Green Stuff, the Gray Stuff and, on patriotic holidays, the Red Stuff.

For a while there was a perky little lady behind the pots whose efficiency and unfailing good humor brightened our noons and diverted our attention from what we were about to eat. But she finally got tired of dishing up the Brown Stuff and went into a different line of work.

One improvises as one must. Today I had a plate of the Gray Stuff with a scoop of Brown Stuff over it. When he heard my order, the man behind me in the line got a giddy look and grasped the railing to keep from going to his knees.

I eat as much as I dare, and the rest I take home, so it is not wasted. Worked lightly into the soil around a tomato plant or rose bush, the Brown Stuff stimulates an absolute frenzy of bloom.

Several years ago, in response to their employees' impudent and small-minded insistence on receiving occasional nourishment, the bosses appointed a food committee to look into the matter. The committee's first action was to throw out the previous lunch room concessionaire, whose offerings included only Gray Stuff and whose representative behind the counter was nagged by a hacking cough.

Other vendors competed for our favors. Meetings were held and presentations made. The briefcases of these ardent suitors were full of gourmet menus. Their manner was ingratiating. None of them coughed.

I served on the food committee. I do not say that immodestly. But it does go to show that, if one works at a place long enough and does one's job and avoids offending one's betters, the honors will come.

A decision was made and a contract awarded. For several months — for as much as a year, even — the improvement was dramatic. Gay cloth streamers were strung over the lunch room entrance. The Brown Stuff was given fancy names, derived from the French. On special days, the serving staff wore costumes and funny hats.

We were fooled into complacency. We forgot to remember that luncheon in the upper room was an event to be feared.

The food committee fell moribund. The brief pretense of democracy was laid aside, and no further meetings were held. I cannot help noticing now that the other committee members avoid the company canteen as they would avoid the green salad in a Guatemalan street cafe.

I still frequent the place. I go at a busy time, when I am sure to be seen, and march through the line slowly, gravely, with a heap of earth-colored victuals steaming on my plate. And I do this for a reason. The mutter of malcontentment has begun to rise again. The mood is turning ugly. In a revolution, there is no knowing whose heads will roll.

When the mobs come rampaging through the corridors, looking for the people who said, "Let them eat Brown Stuff," I want my dish of it in front of me.

SEND THEM TO THE FRONT

I have taken sick to my bed, and as usual in such times I require extensive and almost continuous service. My ailment, however commonplace, is the center of my world and must of course be the center of other people's as well. I want my suffering widely known.

I have never had a trivial illness. They all are profound.

It is not enough that I should sit wan and pathetic through the days. I have also developed a talent for groaning copiously in the night. My ragged sighs and bleats of discomfort reverberate in the dark house, and the wonder is that I can manage to do this even while I am blissfully asleep.

The effect of all this is most satisfactory. My wife, of course, cancels all of her other activities so that she may give herself entirely to the task of restoring my well-being. No one, I am confident, suffers as hugely as I do. My discomfort is unique in its dimensions. That is why I feel justified in making it a public event and the focus of so much attention.

As I write this I sit shuddering, propped on cushions, with the electric blanket turned up to eight. From time to time my wife appears to offer broth or juices. These I reject with a weak wave of the hand and a thin murmur of *"Starve a fever."*

But, it is quite possible that after she has left to discharge some errand on my behalf, I will creep down to the refrigerator to make and wolf a sandwich, enabling me to sustain for a while longer my appearance of joyless decline.

It is the flu that has laid me low. My wife has been subject often to this same disease. And her behavior in those times has led me to a general observation. Which is that women simply do not suffer as men do. Whether the reason is biological or perhaps lies in generations, even centuries, of social conditioning it is impossible to say. In any case, it is obviously true.

For when my wife is sick, I rise and go off to work as usual. As I must. I am concerned for her, naturally, and wish for her speedy recovery. But there is no possible way I can exempt her from the demands of her life. There still is a house to be managed, clothes to be made ready for our use, meals to be prepared, telephone solicitors to be dealt with and her own professional obligations to be met.

And all this she manages to accomplish without complaint. Indeed, often without even comment. As much as a week may pass before, noticing her leaning febrile against a wall for support, I even realize that she is ill. Clearly, she could not continue in such fashion with the routine of her life if her distress in those moments were as great as mine is now.

There seems, then, to be this fundamental difference between the sexes.

Which brings me, however indirectly, to the subject of women's rights. In any discussion of this issue, the opponents of women hold what they believe to be an ace of trumps. Sooner or later they may be depended on to play it with a flourish of triumph.

Where this liberation foolishness is going to end up, they say, *is with women in front-line combat units. And how would you like that!*

Well, I would like that very much. I would encourage it. And I would feel more optimistic about the state of our national defenses and the future of Western democracy as we know it. Men are well-fitted enough for supporting roles, but they feel physical distress too acutely to be suited to the trenches. The ones you want charging the enemy's bunkers and machine-gun nests are the ones that don't feel pain. And, on the evidence, our women could take a lot of lead without complaining.

It is an obscure fact of military history — at least I think it is — that the .45-caliber service automatic was developed specifically for use against Moro warriors who refused to be stopped by conventional firearms of the day. And those Moros were only men. Imagine, then, what it would take to turn a charge of lady Marines? I don't think there's anything in the Russian arsenal that could handle it.

Anyway, that is something reassuring to consider as I lie here awaiting, a little irritably, the constant care and attention that are my due.

KEEPING IN TOUCH

Every day, in traffic, people go whizzing by with one hand on the steering wheel and the other pressing a telephone upside their heads, leaving no hands free to operate the turn signal. The message is clear. They are on the fast track, not just on the street but in life, and it is up to the rest of us to stay out of their way.

I have no real need for such an instrument. Important deals do not come my way. Any business I have to transact can be handled quite satisfactorily by surface mail.

Even so, it makes me uneasy and a little envious to see those people chattering on their car phones. They are people of affairs, while I am a primitive. So to ease the shame I have begun carrying my TV remote control with me when I drive.

In the rush hour, stopped at a traffic signal, I put the thing to my mouth and bark into it an urgent command.

"I want those 600 crates of frozen herring, and I want them fast! Understand?"

Or: *"Get the Saudis on the line and tell them I'm not interested. Venezuela made me a better offer."*

Or: *"This isn't about money. It's about principle. My airline's not for sale."*

The TV control is somewhat smaller and thinner than a real car phone, but the resemblance is close enough. Actually, the size of it may work to my advantage.

The people in the cars beside me will be ringing up their cellular companies and demanding to have one just like it.

"I saw this guy with one this morning," they'll say. "It was a terrific phone — hardly bigger than a TV remote. So find me one like it. This model I've got is obsolete, a piece of junk."

Probably you have been at public events where someone's pager has gone off, telling him to call the office immediately. It's mostly an image thing, suggesting he can't afford to be out of touch even for a minute.

I don't have a pager. What I have is my old pocket-size tape player, and I hardly go anywhere without it. All I have to do is reach in my coat and press the Play button, and it trumpets out the prerecorded beep, followed by a message:

"Prime Minister Blair is asking that you get back to him at your convenience," or, *"You have a message from Tokyo. They need your input on the tariffs."*

I can stand up and rush out importantly. Believe me, in some quiet setting like a theater or a funeral, it's a real attention-getter.

Another contemporary status symbol is the desk telephone with a microphone in it, so you don't have to bother holding the thing — implying the need to keep both hands free for signing contracts, endorsing negotiable instruments and so forth even as you speak.

When some very significant person calls you on one of those, you're never sure whether it is a bad transatlantic connection, or the voice of a prophet coming at you out of a cave.

I hate getting calls like that, and certainly would never own such a device. In any case, it's an unnecessary expenditure. The same effect — the same celestial resonance — can be achieved by holding an empty two-pound coffee can to your mouth while speaking into an ordinary phone.

It isn't so important to actually position oneself on the communications superhighway as it is to appear to be there. And as you can see, there's room on the road for the budget traveler.

MORE ABOUT THE TRIBE

Those genealogy people are at it again, trying to put a heroic face on the Gusewelle clan's contribution to the history of America.

It's a racket, plain and simple. They sit out there someplace with their computer plugged into some humongous database, searching official records in hopes of finding a document — a bankruptcy ruling, notice of parole, *anything* — that mentions the family name.

They probably do this for thousands of names at a time, then their computer cranks out a mass mailing. They toss their bait on the water. And anyone who bites gets reeled in like a carp.

The first book, which I ordered against my better judgment about a year ago, contained some bad disappointments. According to the sections on marriage and military service, the whole bunch of us could pretty much be lumped together as philanderers and shirkers. The way that book had it, not a single Gusewelle ever wore the uni-

form of his country. And only one, in all the recorded generations, ever bothered to make an honest woman of the
mother of his children. The rest of us just lived out our
days in sin.

Now, according to a bulletin in this week's mail, a com-
panion volume is available — a further installment in this
ongoing chronicle of shame.

The notice doesn't say Offer. It says *Invoice* at the top,
and it looks official. I even have my own account number,
AHH4FR. All the previous suckers must get one. So I suppose I will have to cough up the $34.85 or else they might
send a collection agent around to kneecap me or gar-
nishee my check.

I read down the list of subjects this new opus is supposed to contain. One article was titled, "Focus on
Gusewelle Heraldry," and I knew straight away that one
had to be bogus. The Gusewelles back in the "old country"
didn't have coats of arms and such. They rarely had shoes.

Another one was "Gusewelle Family on the Mayflower."
Again, there's a false ring to it. Back in 1620, the year the
Pilgrims put to sea from Plymouth, my German forebears
were not big on travel. It is told in the family how a certain
Great Aunt Huss, who was a Lower Saxon — in fact, the
lowest sort of Saxon — removed the Gusewelle *kinder* from
school to keep them from being exposed to lies about the
roundness of the world.

It is thus ludicrous to suggest that anyone with my
name appeared on the manifest of the Mayflower. In those
ancient times, of our whole brutish tribe, only Cousin
Gerd ever ventured as far as the fetid brook that drained
the swine lot. But from there he could see the village

steeple and smoke from the chimneys and, terrified, he turned back.

In subsequent centuries, it's true, a scattering of Gusewelles did appear on this continent, though how they got here and who let them in is unknown.

I nevertheless put little stock in the chapter titled, "Gusewelle Family on the Oregon Trail." If we were there at all, you can bet it wasn't at the head of a wagon train of pioneers bound for the promise of the West. Lurking off somewhere to the side in the bushes and rocks is where we'd have been, waiting our chance to gun down some straggler and make off with his womenfolk and his goods.

Legend has it that one Alferd Packer, after whom the University of Colorado student grill is named, is the only man in this country ever found guilty of cannibalism. I'd just as soon leave it at that, thank you.

There are some things about the family I'd rather not pay $34.85 to know.

IV

UPS, DOWNS AND ACROSS

Sometimes it's surprising, when toiling over a crossword puzzle, the way arcane bits of knowledge come boiling up out of your subconscious — things you didn't know you knew. Like the word for an Arabian harem room, or the name of some edible seaweed.

Crosswording is a vice my wife and I took up several years ago while living in another country, then weaned ourselves away from, but lately have fallen into again.

I don't know that it really expands one's vocabulary or improves the mind in any useful way, but it provides an excuse for a few companionable minutes together after the supper dishes have been cleared. The other evening, though, our collaboration took a nasty turn.

We'd almost finished the puzzle. Only a few squares were left unfilled.

No. 29 Down had spaces for five letters. The clue was "Men."

"Nerds," said my wife.

I looked up, startled, from the paper.

"Just kidding," she said, with a little laugh.

But she *wasn't* kidding. It had popped out involuntarily — the way, when someone pinches you, you say "Ouch!"

Men.

Nerds.

Let me say that I am neither for men nor against them;

neither deify women nor despise them. Gender has always seemed to me only one fact of a life, and arguably a lesser one.

That women have suffered injustices is beyond dispute. An embittered few of them have taken up the vocation of professional man-hater, making careers of displaying their wounds. But the worthier goal, surely, is fair reconciliation, not partition. For without at least minimal contact between the sexes, it's obvious that this argument — or any other — cannot last for long.

Thus I have let the diatribes wash around and past me, not giving them much importance. Until that moment over the puzzle, that is, when I discovered how wrong I'd been.

Hateful nonsense, repeated often enough, gets a life of its own. In the same subliminal way we know the name of the seaweed without knowing we'd ever learned it, we find one day that the maliciousness has chipped away at our views of one another.

The next puzzle space to be filled was No. 57 Down, for which the clue was "Simpleton." There were four spaces, so Man wouldn't fit.

"It has to be Fool," I said. "Although you could write in Male there and move Fools over to 29 Down, where you wanted to put Nerds. I suppose they're interchangeable."

"Look," she said, "that was only a joke about Nerds. I meant it in fun."

"Sure you did."

We both were bristling a bit.

"Well, shall we finish this or not?" she said. "We only have one left."

"What is it?"

"No. 66 Across. Four spaces. The clue is 'Frost.'"

"Hoar," I said icily.

And then we called a truce.

We had to. If we've learned anything from our years together, it's that solving the crossword — not to mention all the bigger puzzles — is much too hard alone.

HANGING OF THE GREEN

It was the day for putting up the tiny lights and fake greenery that decorate our front doorway in this season, announcing to the neighbors and passing strangers the stupendous happiness of all who dwell within.

Every year this event takes us to the very brink of divorce.

"The greenery isn't even."

"What do you mean, not even? It looks even to me."

"No. There's more on the right-hand side."

"All right, I'll do it again. But this time give me an eye. Don't wait until I'm finished!"

The infernal stuff is taken down and rehung.

"That looks nice," she says.

"Good. Now hand me the lights. We have to end up with the plug on the left side."

Some minutes pass. The lights are nearly up.

"Wait a second," she says. "I think we may have a problem. The plug seems to be on the right."

"*What?* The socket is on the left. I was *counting* on

you!"

"Well, I'm steadying the ladder," she snaps. "I can't do that and everything else, too."

The stepladder is a new 5-foot aluminum model, replacing the rickety wooden one that came with the house 30 years ago. She bought it just last week expressly for this purpose, on the chance it might prevent her from being prematurely widowed. This expenditure was supposed to simplify our public display of merriment. In fact, it has complicated the chore.

"You're standing too high," she says. "You're not supposed to be on that step."

"Why would they put a step there if you can't stand on it?"

"I don't know. But I'm looking right at the sticker under your heel. It says, *Do Not Stand at This Level. Highest Standing Level: 2 feet 10 inches.*"

"That's crazy."

"You'd better read the instructions."

It has never occurred to me that I would require directions for the use of a stepladder.

"Come down and read them anyway," she says.

The various warnings and caveats cover at least four stickers affixed to different parts of the ladder.

FAILURE TO READ AND FOLLOW INSTRUCTIONS, says one of them, in big type, *MAY RESULT IN INJURIES OR DEATH.*

There is a picture showing a man plunging to his death from a height of slightly more than 2 feet 10 inches.

The instructions themselves are in type so small I have to go get my glasses to read them. And they are very elaborate. One says the ladder requires occasional lubrication. Another says to be sure to wear slip-resistant shoes — probably on the chance some lubricant got spilled on the steps.

The ladder is only to be used by someone in good physical condition. And never in front of a door that isn't locked. Not just latched. *Locked,* the sticker says. Also, windy conditions may present special hazards.

"I think we may have to call it a day."

"Why?" she says, her disappointment plain.

"Because I may have on the wrong kind of shoes. And I thought I felt a breeze rising."

"But we're nearly finished."

So we struggled on, and in the end we did get the plastic greenery and the lights up. And I came down from the ladder, feeling lucky to escape with my life.

"Plug in the cord," I tell her. "Pray they come on."

And by some miracle they do — signaling to the world how incredibly joyful we are, and that we're together for at least another year.

FEEDING FRENZY

The neighbor up the block telephoned at an early hour, and I could tell right away there was something terribly wrong. His voice sounded kind of muffled and thin.

"Where are you calling from?" I asked him. "And why are you whispering?"

"I'm in the coat closet with my cell-phone," he said. "I

don't want to risk being heard."

"Are there burglars in the house?"

"No," he said, "it's the doll."

I wasn't sure I'd heard him right.

"Our daughter wanted one of those tickle dolls for Christmas," he said, "but all the stores were out. So we got her a doll that eats stuff instead."

"So what's the problem?"

"It tried to scalp her in the night. We heard her screaming, and barely got there in time."

"It's just a toy," I told him. "All you have to do is switch it off."

"There's no off switch."

"Then take the batteries out."

"Are you kidding? You can't get near the thing."

"So you're alone there?"

"No," he said. "My wife's locked herself and the kids in an upstairs bathroom. I think they're safe for the moment. But I can hear it out there. It ate the shag rug in the family room."

"You're kidding!"

"I'm not either. It goes after anything hairy. The cats can get up high, so they're OK. But I heard some real bad sounds a little while ago. I think maybe it got Shep."

Shep was their collie dog.

"He was barking, going crazy. Then it sounded like a lamp or something fell over, and he kind of whined. After that it got real quiet. Now all I can hear is the clicking it makes when it opens and shuts its jaws."

"Do you want me to call the police?"

"It's no use," he said. "I tried, but they wouldn't come.

They said they don't make toy calls."

"How about the manufacturer?"

"I tried that, too. All I got was a recording with the number of their lawyers. And that number didn't answer."

"I don't know what to say," I told him.

"The bad part is our daughter has some friends coming over to play in about an hour. Maybe you could tape a note to the door, telling them to keep away."

"Sure," I said. "But what about you folks?"

"I guess we'll just have to wait it out."

"How long will that be?"

"I don't know," he said "It came with a year's guarantee."

"You'll never make it."

"Maybe not," he said. "But I'll call you from time to time, if you don't mind. It helps to have someone to talk to."

It was a sad situation, all right.

"Remember how Christmas used to be?" I said. "All we ever wanted was a new ball glove, or maybe a bicycle or something. When they start making things that come after you, I think this toy thing has gone too far."

He didn't say anything.

"Are you still there?" I asked him.

"It's right outside the door," he whispered. "I think it knows I'm here."

"Maybe you could throw it a sweater and make a run for it."

"No use," he whispered. "You wouldn't believe how fast it is."

"Well," I said, "I'll put up that note."

"Thanks."

I could hear the clicking sound over the earpiece of the phone.

"And stay in touch," I told him. "Let me know how it turns out."

I couldn't help thinking how lucky I was that my children grew up before the toy industry came of age.

SONG OF A WINTER TRAIN

The lighted time display on the clock radio said two hours and 25 minutes past midnight — a cheerless hour of morning. I lay abed in the darkness, wondering what sound had wakened me.

Then it came: the lonesome hoot of a train whistle, like a drifter's howl of desolation, flung across the night from some far part of the city to interrupt a dream. Between the whistle's blasts could be heard the thrumming power of the engine, and also — though possibly I only imagined it — the rattle of couplings and the click of wheels on the track.

Fully awake, then, I listened for most of an hour.

A dozen trains passed in that time, maybe more. Some sounded nearer, some farther away. All announced themselves, and the importance of their errands, with the same forlorn hoot.

Sometimes on a night of summer, with the window open beside the bed, I've heard trains calling in the last moment before sleeping or the first after waking. But never have the cries seemed so urgent or so clear. It may be that sound is conducted better, somehow, on the brittle winter air, or that it travels more freely with the trees barren and no foliage to bar the way. You've noticed, perhaps, how far the ringing blows of a woodcutter's ax can be heard through a January woods. The phenomenon must be the same.

Another difference between summer and winter trains is the feeling that the sound of them evokes.

A train whistle in July does not disturb the heart, for it speaks mostly of commerce. A lumbering machine with its cargo of coal or ore, or something else prosaic, is bound for somewhere of no particular interest. Doubtless the journey is of economic significance to someone. But it has nothing to do with your life or with your dreams.

At a hollow hour of a winter night, though, the effect can be troubling, even *transforming*. It starts you thinking . . . of places in the world you've been, and have cared for greatly, and other places you meant sometime to go.

Of chances wasted.

Of the fleetness of time, and the way that inattention lets it get away.

Those are winter thoughts — the kind that come when you're awake at a strange hour, listening to the melancholy song a train is flinging across the lonely dark.

And maybe, as you listen, you experience an epiphany, a life-affecting revelation that changes you for all time. I suppose that must occur sometimes.

Or maybe, as happened with me, the moment passes. And you simply sleep.

PASSION GUIDES THE PEN

My friend writes on, his words precise, his passions keen, even as a world of darkness closes around him.

Diabetes has afflicted him for years, but now his sight is failing faster. I know it from the oversized scrawl of his handwriting on the envelopes that come in the mail, and from his marginal corrections on the proofs of yet another article he is about to publish.

His letter tells that he and his wife will not be coming our way soon. Travel has become difficult. He says it as a matter of fact, without any self-pity.

Nor does his writing touch at all upon his worsening affliction. He is concerned with larger matters: the meaning of family, the decay of traditional values, the plight of a society that seems to him — in several dangerous respects — to be losing, or have lost, its way.

Don't imagine that his is a catalog of pessimism. His belief in the essential American character is great. Implicit in his work is the faith that we can find ourselves again. And he argues his views with elegance, often with humor.

His essays are not widely known. They never have been gathered in a book — though they ought to be. Mostly he is published in scholarly journals, read by a few hundred or a few thousand thoughtful people. His latest piece, beside me here on the desk, was delivered yesterday. I will read it tonight, with humility and something like shame.

Because I know that every idea it contains will be finely turned, every word weighed and chosen. And I will be obliged to consider again what a price some writers must pay simply to do the thing they believe in. While others of us, with no impediment to speak of, gripe endlessly about the hardness of the work.

I had another friend who remained an active writer well past his 100th year. The amazement wasn't just that he managed to live to such an age while continuing to put words on paper, mostly poetry. What struck me was that, to the end, his remained a young man's voice. He mocked the infirmities that overtook him. He celebrated love and was able, even after so long, to greet each season with a fresh eye, as if noticing it for the first time.

Greatness is not to be confused with fame. These two — one of them gone, now, and the other still courageously working — I count among the great writing people I've had the luck to know.

You hear it said that certain writers have a special *gift*. As the word itself suggests, that's a kind of accident. I suppose the gift would be fine, if one happened to have it. But in this line of work — and perhaps in any line — I'm convinced that character and staying power are the surer bets to get one safely through.

WARMED BY LUCK

A bitter wind whispers at the door crack. Sleet rattles like birdshot against the pane. The afternoon gives way to frozen nightfall of a winter arrived too soon, and all creatures alive are divided again into those who have a home to go to and those who haven't.

Yesterday I saw a man in a torn green raincoat — a gaunt man with gray hair flying and strips of blanket bound for warmth around his legs — go in the door of a public library. He had a look of purpose, like someone who couldn't wait to read. But what drew him to that place, you could be fairly sure, wasn't books. It was the hope of a saving hour or two of warmth, before his long ordeal in some lonely corner of the night.

It struck me that although he was not so different, except in luck and circumstance, from a hundred other men I know, he bore no record of his past, and the future could no more be seen in him than in the forlorn birds that fly down stiffly from somewhere to peck and fluff at the feeder.

We keep around us a fairly constant supply of cats and dogs, numbering somewhere between sufficiency and out-right scandal. And most of those, at any given time, have been accidental friends. Anything that presents itself at our door can count on coming in. Its past recedes. Its future assumes the immediate shape of food bowls and beds or radiator tops to sleep upon. Provided, of course, that what appears at the door walks on four legs. Old men in green raincoats with rag-wrapped shins we don't take in.

We think, especially in such weather, of all the cats that haven't come to us. You spy them sometimes, ghosting sharp-ribbed among the crates and cartons of some alley or eyes reflecting at the edge of the car's headlights from the tangled grasses of a winter ditch.

They are all the unnamed, unnumbered kin of the ones we keep and feed. Take them in and in a day, a week, they would be indistinguishable from any of the others, shouldering for a place on the bed's corner, demanding their rations on time.

Just as the homeless staring out of news photographs from some place of pain and ruin are the direct kin of children who sleep between sheets and get braces on their teeth . . .

Just as the gray man in the green raincoat, with blanket-bandaged legs, is no different in any important way from the gray man in necktie and warm topcoat who sees — or doesn't see — him shamble past.

It's the habit of the comfortable and secure to confuse luck with virtue. Whether dogs or cats or men, the ones who have gotten in — the well-fed and warm — listen at the door crack, growling at the footfalls of those others still outside, those less worthy who are passing in the storm.

But virtue's rarely the difference. More often it's blind circumstance that leads some wanderers to safety or, on a sudden cutting winter blast, blows the others by.

THERMALLY CHALLENGED

She prefers a warm room for sleeping. I like cold. It's the kind of niggling little issue from which separations and even monstrous crimes can flow.

We have an electric blanket. One night, some years ago, she turned her dial to 10, and trembled through until dawn. I woke in a febrile stupor.

"You'd better call a doctor," I told her. "I think my malaria's coming back." Then we discovered that somehow, in making the bed, the blanket's controls had gotten switched.

I thought of sleeping in another room. She thought of adding more cats for the body heat they would supply, although the number of cats on the bed already seemed to me sufficient. In the end, we tried to put it behind us and get on together the best we could. But something between us had changed. And I do not allow the blanket to touch me any more, regardless of who's controlling it.

Last week, when the first real spell of chilly weather came, I threw open the window on my side to let the freshness in.

"What are you doing?" she cried.

"Greeting the season," I told her.

"Are you crazy? It's going to be in the 40s."

"I know. And I couldn't be happier."

"We'll freeze."

"You have your blanket," I said. "And you have the cats."

But just then there was a great rush of cats leaving the

bed for some other room in the house where the windows were closed.

"What is this thing you have about sleeping cold?"

"I don't know," I said. And it was the truth. "I think maybe it reminds me of old times — hunting camps and nights in the far north. Things like that."

"I wish I'd known this about you at the start."

"Would it have changed anything?"

"Absolutely! I would have lived in Florida and married a shrimp fisherman."

"Well," I said sleepily. "I guess you're stuck."

"I'm going on a talk show," she said.

"You're what?"

"I'm going on with Oprah or Sally or Donahue and tell everything."

"Those are freak shows. What do you have to tell?"

"I am an abused woman, and the world must hear my story."

"Now wait just a minute!"

"It's true. I am thermally abused."

"That is ridiculous. At most you are seasonally challenged."

"Call it what you like," she said. "I'm cold. And I'm going to drag you through the mud on network TV."

"What if I shut my window halfway?"

"It's a start."

"What if I go bring you some cats?"

"That might warm me a little."

And so we head into another winter — still together, and still hoping to work through our problem without the help of the studio audience.

WHERE'D THAT FOREHEAD GO?

At some point in evolutionary history, around the time the family tree divided — apes on one branch, *Homo sapiens* on another — there's a blank page in the record.

What's absent, scholars contend, is the ambiguous, in-between beast that eventually would be us. They call that the "Missing Link," and generations of scientists have been searching high and low, mostly low, hoping to locate it.

Now they've found it. It turns out to have been a Gusewelle.

At least that's what I see in the latest communique from that outfit that calls itself The Gusewelle Archives. Some time back I made the mistake of sending off for what they advertised as a complete family history. What I got for my money was a sheaf of documents indicating that, as far back as the record went, we Gusewelles have been an unsavory rabble — idlers, draft dodgers, petty thieves, and men who tended not to marry the mothers of their children.

I decided right then I wanted nothing more to do with that genealogy bunch, but they just won't leave me alone. Every few months, now, I get another promotional mailing. The one that came yesterday says that for only $29.99 they will send me their all-new edition of rare and unusual facts about the family, including ancestors, descendants and Gusewelle Missing Links.

Those are the exact words: *Missing Links.*

Let's suppose just for argument's sake it turns out that first sorry creature to climb down from a tree — an unsightly specimen with no chin and a half-inch forehead — really was, in fact, a Gusewelle. I'm not saying it couldn't be true, because every family has a skeleton or two in its closet. But those folks are crazy if they think I'd pay to read about it.

The bonus offer, a $20 value that would come absolutely free along with the Missing Link stuff, is a collection of stories and legends that "humorously paints an historical picture of the Gusewelle Family." What do they mean, humorously? First they say we're subhuman. Now they're going to make fun of us.

The few Gusewelles I have known, my own loved ones excepted, have not by and large been a particularly humorous lot. Over time, we have mostly been country folk, abiding in houses from which the wind had scoured the paint, overlooking hopeless gullied fields. The big event of our day was going out before dinner with a hatchet to deprive a chicken of its head.

Qualitatively, life for many Gusewelles of the modern epoch scarcely has advanced beyond that of the Missing Link. But that doesn't entitle anyone to make us the butt of jokes.

I suppose after this sees print I'll get furious letters from distant Gusewelles — quite numerous, I understand, in Illinois — demanding to know why I've dragged the family name through the mud. They will turn out to be neurosurgeons, bank presidents, theoretical physicists and CEOs of multinational corporations, and they — or their lawyers — will be all over me like ticks on a hound. They'll insist indignantly that this Missing Link business has nothing to do with them. To prove it, they will send snapshots of themselves and their fine-looking children, all with high foreheads and significant chins.

I feel sorry for those people. I don't know how much truth there is in the Gusewelle Family Archives. And I'm certainly not going to shell out $29.99 to own a copy. But I think it's necessary to come to terms with one's heritage, regardless of when one's forebears got an opposable thumb and learned to walk erect.

THEY AREN'T LIKE US

ASPEN, Colo. — The Beautiful People are a breed distinct, like creatures from a different planet.

They turn their skis straight down the mountain at 50 miles an hour, with a look of boredom on their bronze faces. The feet of the Beautiful People never hurt inside their boots.

At the end of the day, they immerse themselves in outdoor whirlpool baths heated to 160 degrees and afterwards roll their long bodies in the snow. Then the Beautiful People go out to restaurants for elaborate and caloric meals which, because their metabolism is different from yours and mine, do not cause them to grow fat.

Finally, they adjourn to the discotheques to dance the night away and form liaisons with beautiful persons of the other gender, and awaken in the morning in strange chalets, without hangovers and with their expressions of boredom intact. (Unlike the rest of us, who would worry about such things as our toothbrushes, Beautiful People do not have morning breath.)

It is a closed society, and very hard to crack.

I have come here with a group of men who annually take this brief recess from job and family to ski and to work at being Beautiful People. In my opinion it is useless. This is only my second year, but some of them have been coming 15 seasons now and, while they are fine sports and good company, they still have not become beautiful in any socially important sense of that word.

Speaking at least for the seven of us lodged together in this apartment, we do not wake up in the mornings in strange beds. That is never even a serious danger. We pass along the same streets used by the Beautiful People. We appear on the same mountain. We eat sometimes in the same restaurants, although rich food at this altitude does not rest kindly on our stomachs. There is even rash talk about staying until the closing hour at the Paragon Ballroom — but that is rarely, if ever, done.

If truth were known, I doubt that the Beautiful People even notice we are here. Any more than it would occur to them, while passing in airplanes between Aspen and the East Coast, that there might actually be intelligent life somewhere below them in the trackless mid-region of the continent.

The differences between us are simply too vast.

For one thing, our feet — unlike theirs — do hurt inside our ski boots. They hurt terribly. After breakfast we all array ourselves in what we imagine to be our Beautiful People costumes and sit down in chairs to draw on and buckle boots. It is the most intense moment of the day. Faces go blank. There is a profound silence as each contemplates the private dimensions of his pain. Then we go to the mountain.

Some of us fall down in the lift line or otherwise abase ourselves, temporarily impeding the Beautiful People on their way to pleasure. But once having ridden the lift to the top, it is possible to enjoy a spell of fine democracy. For, sitting at an outdoor table of the Sundeck Restaurant on the summit of Aspen Mountain — ringed by glittering peaks and drinking bad wine overpriced — almost anyone can imagine himself beautiful. It is best to prolong that moment, because eventually it will be necessary to ski down.

We do not turn our skis down the mountain at 50 miles an hour. Our purpose in coming here was not to get to know orthopedic surgeons and physical therapists on a first-name basis. When we stand poised at the head of some steep run, looking down on the rooftops of Aspen like an aerial photograph below, the expression that passes over our faces would never be mistaken for boredom.

Dread manifests itself in different ways. I have noticed that my feet contract to the size of walnuts inside the hated boots, and I am like a bird frozen to the wire. In such moments, as I consult the trail map for an alternative way down — a service road, perhaps — it is plain to me that beautiful personhood simply is not in the cards. I have started too late. The way is too long, and life too short.

Not so, perhaps, for the physician friend who happens to be my roommate on this trip.

I have noticed that he has begun to speak less about the discomfort of his feet. Last night he put himself through the ordeal of the hot whirlpool and the roll in the snow and declared it wonderful — though he looked a little drawn.

Afterward he went out to dinner. It is reported that he closed the Paragon.

For him, there may still be time.

THE SURVIVALIST

As with any other aboriginal man, winter is my time of pride.

Our food cache is full of the rigid corpses of creatures caught or slain in the sweeter season. The northers may howl for a month without respite. The way to the supermarket may become drifted and impassable. But by my great cleverness, hunger will be kept from our lodge.

Do our arteries crave red meat? "Venison, woman," I say. Literary custom mandates that aboriginal men must address their mates as woman.

Does lighter flesh appeal? "Fish," I command. "We will eat fish from the shining blue waters."

Actually, the waters I frequent in summer range from murky to coffee brown. But with the passage of a little time, that can be overlooked. A catfish is pretty much a catfish. Carp is carp.

Last night we had a mess of quail. In sherry sauce. A mess of quail is an oxymoron. By rights it should be called an *elegance* of quail, since hardly anything is finer for the table. My experience is a bit limited. I have not eaten dog, rattlesnake, endangered sea turtle, canaries or hundred-year-old Chinese duck eggs. But of the things I've tried, quail are tops.

We put the birds in our aboriginal French clay cooker, slipped the vessel into our primitive but functional microwave and stood, giddy at the odors, waiting for the buzzer to sound.

After our dinners of venison, fish and quail, there is a goose. I didn't shoot the goose, but it was my wisdom to cultivate as a friend the man who did. After the goose, there's a wild turkey. After the turkey, there's a brace of grouse. After the grouse, there's a rabbit.

My woman draws the line at rabbit, and this one is very old — so old that I forget exactly how it was gotten. Or why. It may have been road kill. Anyway, it has been in the freezer several years, now, and has the color and feel of plywood. But at least if spring is late and our stores run low, the rabbit is there for consideration.

There also may be two or three duck breasts. Carbon dating would show them to be from 1983, which is when I got the bird dog, Rufus, and gave up ducks for quail. So they are last in line, even after the rabbit.

I'm not unaware that this whole discussion must be extremely distasteful to the anti-hunting people who regard all creatures in nature as equal in every way. If men eat partridges, they ask, why shouldn't partridges eat men? And I confess to not having the answer, although as far as I know it has never happened.

The fact that deer and hares and quail love and lust in a free and natural state seems, in the view of those folks, to make the slaying and eating of them somehow nastier. It is quite different with cows and chickens which, in this modern day, as is well-known, enter the world already prepackaged in family portions, shrink-wrapped on styrofoam trays.

But never mind argument. We live as we live — savagely. The hardness of our lives and of the climate requires it. Last night, after the quail in sherry, I stepped out coatless into the yard for a few minutes. The cold wind came raking, but I wasn't even chilly. Enough wine in the casserole will do that to you.

I could not help thinking, then — although modestly, of course — how incredibly lucky is any family to have such a provider. "Come in, Nanook," she called from the door. "You'll catch your death."

But I was one with nature. My belly was warm and full, and so was my woman's. And I pretended not to hear.

THE FEBRUARY TRAP

Like zircons and miracle diets and bundles of Confederate bonds found in an attic footlocker, these days of middle February are wonders of empty promise.

The creaking of the ancient furnace subsides. The mornings come clear, and the twilights are softest lemon behind the trees. Buds visibly swell. Locked spirits loosen, and spring seems near.

It is a time when I am glad to be a man creature, with my memory of winters past and a calendar to show the way. Instead of, say, a mouse creature — its experience bounded by a single season, empty of any longer wisdoms, imagining the year's turn in the first sweet spell of false warming.

Keep a cabin in the woods, as I do, and you will learn, among other things, the habits of mice. They materialize with the frost — come from somewhere, from under leaves, from out of their tunnels in the bent grass — to gain a surer shelter. Their seeking is all but irresistible.

Somewhere between the foundation stones they will find a crevice. Or, where two boards do not perfectly join, the crack will be enlarged by an eternity of patient gnawing. In waves they come, and nothing I know of will turn them.

The actual damage they do has always seemed to me exaggerated. A page of newspaper — not enough to start a stove fire, and bearing only antique news about the world, if any news at all — may be shredded to make a provident nest. Food in tins or in glass jars is safe enough. A bar of soap might be eaten and, heaven knows, if hunger comes to that, they're welcome to it.

Then, in spring, after the ice has left the pond but before the birdfoot violets or the first peeping of frogs, they are gone again. Not gone by stages, but vanished all at once, as secretly as they came. Ten minutes with a broom and dust pan erases any memory of their having been there.

But when, if you happen to be a mouse, is the exact moment for going?

Remember, now, that you have never seen a spring before. Between the first blind squirming and the final shadow of the owl, a year is an eternity. No cumulative wisdom of your kind speaks to you. You have no means of numbering the days. You proceed without advice.

When is spring, then? Is it when the light grows moderately longer — or can that be noticed in the dungeon corner of some bureau drawer? Is it when survival no longer must be sought among the trembling, close-pressed bodies of your confreres? Or when the days grow mellow, the wind swings into the south and the afternoon sun warms every stone, is that finally spring?

I remember very well, several years ago, just such a spell of February weather. You may recall it, too.

Winter was canceled. With friends, we took our children to the park for a cookout and lingered, all of us in shirt sleeves, until long after dark. It was a freakish kind of gift that could not last. But it did last. Spring bulbs burst up eagerly through the crusted ground. Lawns prematurely greened. Flowering bushes and trees washed the world with color.

Then, in a single night, the wind wheeled round again and winter came raging back with a howl of horizontal sleet. The temperature sank off the chart. The earth went hard as pavement; the bright foliage turned brown as old leather. And the furnace groaned once more. Another month of that we had.

There's hazard in being quite so easily deceived.

That spring there were fewer blossoms.

For several years afterward there were fewer mice.

MONSTROUS GOODNESS

It may be taken as a general rule that spectacular crimes are committed only by the nicest people. Either that, or heinous deportment somehow reveals in those people an excellence of character that previously had gone unremarked and uncelebrated.

A lifetime spent reading the news of unlawful and often violent behavior leads to no other possible conclusion. Let some fellow burn down an old-age home and afterward go rampaging naked through a campsite of horrified Girl Scouts, and the next day's paper will be full of testimony from his neighbors and fellow congregants to the effect that he is an exemplary family man and pillar of his church.

"It simply can't be Baldwin," they say. *"The police must have the wrong man."* But there he is in the photographs — good old Baldwin, none other — in *flagrante delicto* among the scattered cookware and tumbled tents.

When an ingenious embezzlement has brought a company to ruin, its assets siphoned off to be squandered in the casinos and fleshpots of Rio by some bespectacled clerk, can you remember a case — even one — when the malefactor's former associates did not say of him, *"Why, this job was his life!"* Or when the president of the ruined firm did not add, effusive and amazed, *"He was the soul of loyalty, Smidly was. I never had a finer employee."*

If I happen to open the page to a news story whose lead paragraph begins by describing some 35 year-old man as "a sensitive, considerate son, altogether devoted to his mother," I know it is unnecessary to read further. The rest will only recite the horrific details of what he did to her with an ax or a ballpeen hammer.

This recurrent oddity — the astonishing goodness of people who do alarming things — was brought freshly to mind by an event not many days ago. A citizen with a past record of peace disturbance, disorderly conduct and unlicensed driving led police on a high-speed car chase, crashing finally into another car, then leaping from the wreck and fleeing into a nearby apartment whose female resident he took hostage and from whose windows he fired pistol shots and screamed obscenities at the surrounding officers.

The episode ended about as well as could be hoped. The man's hostage escaped — hurt, but not dangerously so. And the author of the rampage was eventually captured in the apartment without having to be dispatched.

The headline of a subsequent story described him, on the word of his friends, as "quiet and talented." The text went farther, reporting him to be, in fact, *"a perfect gentleman."* Of course, I thought to myself. What other sort of person would have done what he did?

No doubt there are other people at large, perhaps even quite a few of them, who also are quiet, talented, gentlemanly and, like Baldwin and Smidly, exemplary citizens and model employees. The pity is that their lights remain hidden under bushels. The excellence of their character is, for the moment, unrecognized.

Although in time we may expect to hear more about them.

V

FAR TRAVELERS

NAPLES, Fla. — It's said this is an indifferent season for finding seashells. Offshore currents hold them in the deeps, or carry them off to other shores. Earlier, we're told, is when the finest ones come in.

No matter. *Now* is when we're here. So when the tide is low, we're out patrolling, awash to our shanks at the edge, glad for whatever modest treasures the inbound swells throw up.

Mostly they're the common ones. Their names come back to us like a language once known but long unused. The turkey wing and jewel box clams, the murexes and whelks, the augers and Scotch bonnets and nutmegs and lettered olives and shark's-eye snails.

We're at it until the sun beats down hard and the waves of the rising tide begin to crest and break, churning up a murk of sand and grit in which nothing can be seen. Then we retreat indoors and spread our gatherings on towels in vain display. And wait for late afternoon and the falling tide again.

We are less discriminating now than we were the last time, which was a dozen years, or maybe longer, ago. That was in the month of March, a season of great abundance. And we would keep nothing with a flaw of any kind. Shelves and bowls and window ledges of our midlands home filled up with the unblemished specimens we carried back.

In some way, though, the passage of time has changed us — made us more forgiving of imperfection.

One day there was a great abundance of shells crusted over with barnacles. There's no telling what event far out in the gulf's waters caused them all to come in together. I passed those up, but my wife kept a good many in her collecting sack. And, for a fact, when they were laid out afterward for inspection, they were of considerable interest.

Even broken pieces can be worth attention.

Sometimes, at the eye's corner, you spy tumbling in the shallows just a palm-sized fragment that, from the fluting of its edges, you know must once have been part of some immense shell of a kind you've never seen before. You can imagine what a splendid thing it surely was. You wonder what creature made it. And how many hundreds or thousands of miles it has ridden with the current to make landfall at your feet.

Yes, it's broken. But what does that matter? Doesn't time break everything finally?

For man or mollusk, the journey is long, the abrasion fierce. In the end, the important thing is what we've been — not what the waves' churning has reduced us to. So naturally the fragment goes in the sack with the others.

There are, we've decided, no unworthy seashells — only some that have traveled harder and farther than the rest.

SEEKING THE LIGHT

NAPLES, Fla. — It's hard to leave paradise — and even harder this time, when three of us will be bound for home while the other, the daughter working in New York, will be headed her different way. I remember an African friend once saying, *"Distance is dangerous."* You feel that most acutely when children grow and leave.

The clock chirped its alarm at an early hour on this morning of our going, and I rolled from bed in darkness to make coffee and begin putting things in a suitcase in readiness for the plane.

I'd switched on the kitchen light and started the kettle heating on the stove, when I heard soft tapping at the sea-facing glass wall of the next room. I went out on the balcony to investigate, and found a little bird fluttering there, trying to make its way indoors.

What brought it there, so high above trees and sea, I couldn't say. Most likely it was drawn, like a moth, to the light. Nor do I know what kind of bird it was. Small as the least of the finches, it had dark wings and back, a somewhat paler underside and an orange bib at its throat.

It batted at the glass a few moments longer. Then, exhausted or just hopeless, it dropped to the floor of the balcony and let itself be gathered up. From far below came the hiss of waves breaking on the sand. The moon was full and still a hand's-breadth high in the west, but it would be most of an hour, yet, before the morning light.

The little bird lay quietly in my cupped hand, either in

contentment or more likely in resignation. I stroked the small head with my forefinger, and wondered if it had injured itself against the pane.

Then, because there was nothing else to do, I told it, "Go, bird" — said the words aloud — and gave it a little toss from the balcony's rail. Instantly it was back, though, fluttering at the glass, seeking the light of the room inside.

Strangely, I found myself thinking in that moment of my daughters, just launched into the world, and of myself at that age. And of how all of us are drawn to the brightness of our illusions, never understanding the hazards that can wait along the way. What's the help for it? None, I suppose. The hope is only to stay aloft long enough, without too many hurts, until at last the real day comes.

So I picked the little bird up again. But this time I carried him around to the far side of the balcony, away from the bright window. From there, all that could be seen was the white curve of the beach below in the moonlight, and the many-colored sparkle of distant buildings farther south along the shore. "Go now," I said again, and opened my hand.

And quick as an eye-blink, he was gone into the safety of the dark.

THE SOLITARY

The black cat, Headlight, decided in kittenhood to pass his life in a state of high alert. Surveying the world, he saw nothing and no one to be trusted. So he dedicated himself to remaining a creature apart.

He would rest only when the others of the household were safely asleep. At all other times, the gold coins of his eyes would shine as wide and round as headlights. If a hand reached out to stroke him, he would dodge it as you'd dodge a blow.

He is a formidable creature. If you had come upon him at large in the woods, you'd have thought perhaps he had escaped from a traveling circus. But his timidity was even greater. If anyone were foolish enough to try to pick him up, he would splay his paws, unsheath his knives and make himself as lovable as a bramble thicket or a roll of concertina wire.

If spoken to, he would withdraw to some other room. His preference, in fact, was not even to be looked at. Those other cats could take all the risks they wanted, but he meant to play it safe.

That was two years ago, and there was a lot he didn't know. He didn't yet understand the high probability that the whine of the electric can opener meant that a tin of tuna was about to be shared. Or that shrimp on the night's menu was another event for general celebration.

He didn't know — until he slipped through a door left carelessly ajar and spent a rainy night under a bush somewhere, alone — that too much company can be better than none at all. He hadn't counted on the congeniality of the others under that roof, nearly all of them with histories of the street.

It took awhile to understand that every collision with a heavy foot is not deliberately intended, and that if you're a black cat against a black floor in a dark hall, you have some responsibility in traffic.

The changes have been gradual and grudging. We have not courted him. We've let him find his own way. First, he began to show an inclination to spend time in a room where people were — though in the farthest corner of it. One day he answered to his name. Another day — after something like a year had passed — he took the awful risk of joining someone in a chair. His own boldness horrified him. His pupils were dilated like a gunfighter's, and you could tell he regretted it immediately.

From then on, the transformation has been swift.

If he happens to be on a counter when someone passes, he reaches out a claw to catch a shirt or sweater — just to announce, in case anyone is interested, that he is there and available.

Yesterday, as I was standing by a morning window, he came up from behind on silent feet and flung himself against my legs with such force that I had to stumble to regain my balance. (He's a significant cat: nearly 20 pounds, and still eating.)

He may never tolerate being held or carried. Even now, as he's being stroked, some old memory will come to him and he'll suddenly cringe and slink away, ashamed of the docile thing he's become. Basically, I have to say, I think he's right about the world. It's a dangerous place. Let your guard down, and you never know where the blow will come from. The deepest wounds result from misplaced trust.

But the solitary life — I can say from the experience of one who long ago tried it — is no bargain either. You mean to be a fighter, always on your guard. Then too many things go right and love intrudes, and without quite knowing how it happened, you lose your edge.

AWAITING A LITTLE LUCK

Wherever the women of my household go, cats present themselves — creatures of uncommon excellence, and all of them needy. The other morning it was my daughter, telephoning from her work. "There's this kitten," she said.

The words caused my breathing to become rapid and shallow. Our need for additional cats is not great. "It was outside the garage where I park," she said. "Next door to a homeless shelter. The men there have been taking care of it. It's a sweet kitty, and very friendly."

"Yes, I'm sure."

"I asked one of the men if he'd keep it until you got there."

"Until *what?*"

"He said he would. You'll know the place. You'll see a group of fellows on the sidewalk out front."

Time has taught me the uselessness of protesting. So of course I drove there, and, as promised, several men were talking together outside the doorway of the shelter. But the prize beast was nowhere to be seen, and for the briefest moment my heart leapt up.

I parked the car and approached the men. They were chatting amiably in the cool of morning — men of different races, but bound together by that comradeship of people who've lost their way or lost their luck.

"My daughter called about a cat," I said to one of them.

"Sure," he said. "The cat. It's here somewhere."

"He wants the cat," another said.

News of my mission circulated among them. "Where's the cat? He was here a minute ago."

"It's a little tomcat," the first man said. "I think maybe he's in the garage."

That was where they kept his food dish and his water. One of the men went in the garage and returned a moment later with the cat in the crook of his arm. As advertised, it was a handsome little fellow, about half-grown — a gray and black tabby with fine, clear markings, and wonderfully amiable. "Your daughter wants him, does she?"

"Well, it's really up to you," I said.

"Sure," a man said. "Take him. He needs a place."

I got the box from the car. "You're sure you don't mind?"

"No. Go ahead."

They helped me put him in the box. "There's some food back there if you want it."

"No," I told them. "We have some cats already. There's food at home."

I felt bad afterward about not taking it. It was what they

had to give. "I'm glad someone's going to look after that little cat," one of the men said.

"We'll get him checked out at the vet's. Get him his shots."

"Good. He's a good cat."

I put the box in the car, thanked them, and I drove away with him, then — a cat who'd found his home and his luck, leaving those men standing on the sidewalk, still waiting for theirs.

JUST LOOK AT THE FACES

Those of us who meet each weekday morning in the line at the doughnut shop treat one another with kindness and elaborate deference.

If a young woman requires the comfort of a half-dozen glazed twists before going off to the purgatory of the steno pool, surely it's her affair. If a middle-aged journalist prefers to face life with a brain besotted by warm dough, whose business is that?

Sometimes the line stretches out onto the driveway, but we remain orderly. The etiquette of the queue is strictly observed. I cannot say how we would respond if some newcomer, all pushy and brusque, were to try to slip through the doorway and insinuate himself ahead of his proper turn. It has never happened.

The only possibility of disorder has to do with the doughnuts — how many of them, and of which variety, can be seen waiting plump on the racks as one nears the front of the line.

Say your specific and very keen desire is for devil's-food. Or applesauce. Or jelly-filled. Never mind which. Suffice that it is a selective addiction. And suppose that, of the ones you must have — jelly-filled, for argument's sake — only six remain on the tray.

You eye the people ahead ahead of you in the queue and seek to divine their likely preferences. That one surely must be a bear-claw type. His workman's dress suggests a need for weight and volume. The one behind him is a delicate young thing, and very stylish. She would go for color, perhaps the pink-iced. And so forth — trying, in each case, to determine how their wants might impinge on your own satisfaction.

Now you are nearly to the front of the line. It is the lady's turn ahead of you. She is a lady of a certain girth. No stranger, that one, to this place. Her eye passes casually over the display. "I'll need a couple of dozen," she says. And the boy behind the counter waits ready with the box. "It doesn't much matter," she tells him. "They're for the office. Just throw in some long johns and some caramel rolls and some of those sugared ones." The boy's hands fly nimbly among the trays. "And while you're at it," she says with hateful indifference, "you might as well let me have that last half dozen jelly-filled."

Your knees go loose and a sound can be heard rising in your throat — a sound that is not pretty. You find yourself praying that you will never look out over the dashboard of your car and see that woman, with a box of doughnuts, crossing in the pedestrian lane. But you do not make a scene. Civility in the line is the unspoken rule.

There are other protocols. In the line at the doughnut shop, one does not speak of diets. We have not come there to be reminded of celery and grapefruit and the Scarsdale doctor in his livelier days. Neither does one let oneself be noticed looking too closely at the physiques of one's companions in the queue.

I have looked surreptitiously, of course. We all have. It is, I have to say, a spectacle worth observing. But mostly when we look at one another it is from the neck up. Our eyes meet, with understanding and not without a sort of tenderness. One sees good nature there, and forgiveness, and, most of all, a surpassing contentment.

Doughnut eaters, as you know if you have ever stood in that line, have beautiful faces.

SHORT, DOESN'T DANCE

I am at ease, perfectly at ease, with crumbling stereotypes and with equality, real equality, of the sexes. I applaud the changes yesterday brought. I welcome the ones tomorrow may bring.

Having said that, I am not sure I am quite ready yet for a woman who advertises herself in the singles classified columns as *"dynamic and dangerous."* And who follows threat with gratuitous insult, saying, *"Short men need not apply."* That's exactly how she put it.

Even if one is not presently single, it does no harm to keep abreast of the literature. The time might come when, like an aging relief pitcher, one would need to test one's value in the marketplace.

But what I see in the ads is not encouraging.

Leanness seems to be much in demand. Leanness, sincerity, abstemiousness about tobacco, financial security and the ability to dance. Inarguably, all of those are virtues. But reading down the list of them, I do not find myself described.

Here, in one of the advertisements, is a DWFGLGBGPA (divorced white female, good looking, good body, good personality, affectionate) who says, *"Just like Uncle Sam, I'm looking for a few good divorced men."* How many are a few? How many are enough? Is the lady insatiable? It is immaterial. She specifies that her army must be composed of fellows over 5 feet 8 inches in height. And I lack an inch of being qualified to enlist.

For reasons sufficient to me, for which I do not apologize, I generally skip over the ads placed by men. But two in a recent paper caught my eye. One seeks a response from someone interested in making fudge together. *"Each lick half the bowls,"* it promises. A kinky proposal if I ever heard one. Another man writes that he hopes to meet a woman who is *"not too flirty and who doesn't talk dirty."* The poor devil may have been through a lot — left in the lurch by roving-eyed tootsies who swore like parrots — but at least his message is arresting.

I would have less to work with.

> SGMNLDD (short gray male, not lean, doesn't dance) sleeps in chair. Burns holes in suits and carpet, works irregularly, licensed to hunt in four states, has five shotguns, three dozen decoys, outboard motor, seeks sincere companion for frozen mornings in the field. Permanent relationship possible.

That's the most appealing sort of ad I could honestly

write. And my phone would be rung off the hook by single women trying to give away their ex-husbands' Labrador retrievers.

The sexual revolution has swept away taboos. Marriage now is seen as but a way station on the road to total self-discovery. The magazine racks and book shelves are heavy with works celebrating the joys of living alone.

Yet, strangely, not only is there still loneliness, but loneliness seems to have become a growth industry. And the literature it produces, at least in the classified columns, remains the stuff of tears. "Henry, come home," the ads used to say. "I still love you."

Now they say: "*Anyone* come home. I might learn to love you."

Except for short men, who need not apply.

OUT OF THE ICE AGE

Our cars are more or less of the recent sort. We have come to terms with computers, mastered the operation of the cassette player, learned to set a digital clock.

Superficially, we pass as moderns. But in our souls we are prisoners of another time. We both are children of the Great Depression, imprinted by parents for whom thrift was a survival virtue and waste the most contemptible of sins. We cannot throw away food.

Yesterday my wife discovered in the upper compartment of the refrigerator a frozen package of something that, when unwrapped, resembled fish. No clue how it had come to us, or from where. Suffice that it once had been meant to be eaten and therefore probably still could be.

It became our supper.

When thawed, it had the look of fish. And the smell of fish. But its texture was strangely elastic. Cooking would not break it down. "The recipe says to microwave it two minutes on full power," my wife read from the book. "Then turn it, and cook two to four minutes more — until it flakes."

We zapped the object the prescribed time. "Does it flake?" she asked.

"No," I said. "I can't drive a fork into it using both hands."

"Let's give it another two minutes."

"Two minutes won't touch it. It's like a truck tire."

A nice curry sauce helped, but the atmosphere at table was somber as we tried to hack the thing into pieces that could be swallowed. It didn't matter so much that we couldn't eat it all. The moral point was that we had tried.

That was from the upstairs refrigerator, whose contents turn over on the average of every year or two. The chest freezer in the basement holds far stranger artifacts.

In holiday seasons, when the price of turkeys slides away to pennies, we usually buy several of the biggest we can find. In any reasonable system, these would be rotated toward the top. We have no system. The only accurate way to establish the true age of the lower turkeys would be through carbon dating. Time and the desiccating cold do their work. Then, periodically, one of those surfaces in the shuffle — a bird the size of a Volkswagen, weighing less than a Cornish hen.

Worst are the frozen blocks wrapped in brown paper and labeled "Farm Beef."

I try to calculate when last we slew a calf. To the best of my memory, it was in the early 1980s, although it could have been the last of the '70s. We look at those packages sidelong, the laws of our upbringing at war with naked fear. "We should get rid of that stuff," we tell each other. Then we remember the accounts of early travelers who, coming upon the corpses of mammoths preserved in the permafrost of the polar regions, thawed and ate the ancient flesh, declared it palatable, and suffered no reported ill effects.

We also remember the stories of our childhood — of crowds milling outside the padlocked banks and brokers standing on the building ledges. "Maybe we'll keep it a little longer," we say, and hide the beef deeper under the strata of weightless turkeys. "Just in case there's some emergency."

Sure enough, there is an emergency. It's now. We're it. Care to drop by for dinner sometime?

SMELL IT AND TREMBLE

I was passing innocently through a department store on my way to neckties when a young woman sprang out from the shadow of the escalator. Times being what they are, naturally I threw up my hands and waited for her to take my wallet.

I'm a liberal on the equal opportunity issue. And it

gave me a certain ideological satisfaction to know I was about to be robbed, or maybe worse, by a woman mugger. But all she did was hand me a scented card and a small envelope. My karma for the day did not include an assault. What had happened was that I'd stumbled unaware into a point-of-purchase giveaway.

I examined the things she'd pressed upon me. They were promotional items for *Lust,* a new fragrance for men. It was available, the card said, in no fewer than 10 preparations to be sprayed, sprinkled, dusted or smeared on the body, or absorbed in the bath.

The odor of the card itself was incredibly powerful. It stank like anything. "What do I do with this?" I asked the young woman.

"Put it in your pocket."

I opened the envelope. Inside was a tiny vial of fluid. "You don't have to tell me," I said. "I carry it in my mouth, like a cyanide capsule. And if I get lonely, I crush it between my teeth."

"Huh?"

From her expression, she thought I was some kind of wacko. "Just a joke," I assured her.

"*Lust* is nothing to joke about," she said seriously. "It could change your life."

"I don't want my life changed. I only came in here for a necktie, not a total retooling."

"You have a closed mind."

"If that's your opinion, you're entitled to it."

"And you're also very rude."

"Look," I said,"I didn't start this. You did."

"All we're asking is that you try it. Carry the card in

your pocket."

"What if I meet someone I know?"

"Almost anything could happen."

"That's what I'm afraid of," I said. "Suppose I just carry it until I get out of the store."

"It's a deal. Have a nice day."

Moving in a strong and faintly phosphorescent nimbus of *Lust*, I walked on toward men's wear, where a clerk approached. "I'm looking for a necktie," I told her.

"Any particular kind?"

"One without gravy on it."

The sales clerk seemed flustered. "My goodness!" she said. Perspiration suddenly beaded her lip. Her voice trembled and her breath came in ragged gasps.

"What is it?" I asked. "Are you ill?"

"It's that smell," she said. "I feel funny all over."

I will not speak of what happened back there among the racks of neckties and shelves of dress shirts. All I can say is that the clerk and I were not responsible — the perfume people were. And I feel sure their lawyers will be hearing about it shortly.

TWO HEARTS JOINED

The recent arrival of Stripe, the gray tabby kitten from the homeless shelter, has upset the delicate equilibrium of our tribe and provoked a chorus of outraged singing among the established residents.

If you've ever kept cats, you know that the ones with seniority never are pleased to have a newcomer among them.

Ugly sounds were made. Blows were struck. Stripe, though small, was a survivor from the street, not easily daunted. But the lack of cordiality must have mystified or even saddened him a bit.

He'd begun life as a loner, of course. As had the great black misanthrope, Headlight — his nature disfigured early by something that he is unable to speak about, and we cannot hope to know.

Then a strange thing happened.

The two of them — Stripe and Headlight — found their way to one another. There's no guessing how or why, for one is feisty and combative, the other stolid and fearful, with a panther's body but a mouse's heart.

It's said, sometimes, that opposites attract. Or perhaps they sensed their common histories of aloneness. One day they were found sprawled close together on the couch. A day or so after that they were sleeping together in a tangle, waking from time to time for some reciprocal grooming. Stripe, being small, does not require much maintenance. But washing Headlight is an ongoing job for the little cat. The great golden eyes slide closed in pleasure as that attention is received.

Our intention was that the kitten's lodging here would be temporary, only until our daughter could find an apartment where he'd be welcome. But now I see the plan is fatally flawed. Those two, the solitary and the newcomer, have found a meeting of the hearts that seems somehow to be a comfort against less happy times remembered.

So it's clear. Both will have to go with our daughter, or both will have to stay. In this uncertain world, a friendship like that, however improbable, is too valuable to let get away.

THE CLOTHES HORSE

Every decade or so my shabbiness becomes a family issue, and I am driven out — a sale circular stapled to my sleeve — with orders to darken the door of some clothing store. Yesterday was that wretched day. "Can I help you?" asked the clerk, an anorexic looking lad of about 25.

"It's possible," I told him. "I am commanded by the woman I live with to buy a sports jacket."

"Did you have a color in mind."

"Something inconspicuous. My taste does not tend toward flamboyant displays."

"Try on this navy blazer," said the clerk. "It may be the only one we have in your size."

He held the coat while I thrust my arms into the sleeves. Then he spoke the dreaded words: "Step over here to the 3-way mirror." I hate 3-way mirrors. They are instruments of comic humiliation that belong in a carnival funhouse. No man past middle age ought ever to have to stand in front of one. "How does it feel?"

"It seems to fit all right," I told him. "What size is it?"

"It's a 44," the clerk said. "Forty-four Short Portly."

I mastered a powerful impulse to hit him in the mouth. "Listen," I said, "I came in here to conduct a civil transaction. Forty-four is unkind enough. *Short* is a gratuitous editorial comment. *Portly* is unforgivable."

"We used to call it Stout."

"Perhaps you don't realize it, young man," I told the clerk, "but you are on very thin ice."

He saw I was serious. "Now, rather than bloody your lip, I will just step outside the store and come back in, and we will try this again from the beginning."

"Yes, sir," said the clerk.

I went out and re-entered. "Can I show you something?" he asked.

"Yes. Something in a sports jacket. And in discussing size, I suggest you avoid use of the P word. Bear in mind you are looking at a man who used to weigh 145 pounds dripping wet."

"*Heh!*" said the clerk.

"Beg pardon?"

"Nothing, sir. I think we might have one jacket cut slender enough."

"Would it by any chance be blue?"

"Well, yes, as a matter of fact, it's —"

"I'll take it."

"Would you like to have a look in front of the mirror?"

"I said I'll take it," I told him. "Don't push your luck."

"How about some pants to go with that coat?" said the clerk.

He was only doing what he'd been trained to do. "Light charcoal, maybe. With an elastic waist."

"You're a model of tact," I said.

"I don't understand."

"Obviously not. But someday you will say that to the wrong person, and you will find yourself in a hospital bed, in traction."

"I guess that means you don't want to try on the pants."

"You're right," I told him.

On state occasions I will be arrayed now in this garment tailored for a stranger. It looks wonderful, according to my wife. But looking wonderful takes more effort, and a thicker skin, than I seem to remember it once did.

FOUR MIGHT BE A CROWD

A recent advertising supplement offered readers a few do-it-yourself decorating tips, little touches to make the house more livable.

Such things as how to make a kitchen brighter and more spacious, or the window treatments more elegant, or the grounds a bit more inviting. Among them were some ideas for sprucing up the bathroom.

One suggestion was an oversized bathtub whose dimensions would make it suitable for use by anywhere from two to as many as four persons at once. Shocking, isn't it, what you can come across in a family newspaper apt to be seen even by young persons of tender years — and on a Sunday at that!

I don't mean to sound prudish. I know there are all different kinds of lifestyles, and I wouldn't pretend for a minute that mine is better than anyone else's. But any historian can tell you that gang bathing was to blame for the fall of Rome and the decline of the Pittsburgh Steelers.

And just offhand I'm unable to think of any three other persons with whom I'd be inclined to share a tub.

I grew up severely disadvantaged — the only child in a family of two parents, a fox terrier and two box tortoises, with but one bathtub for the six of us. It was taken for granted that we would occupy that fixture singly. Ignorant of the more socially liberated habits of the Hollywood stars, we thought that was how everyone lived. The first time I saw a shower — or even heard of such a thing — was when I got to high school and discovered I had to go out for football if I wanted to use one with any regularity.

Limited by these early childhood experiences, I have been content to spend the greater part of the rest of my life in apartments and houses with only tubs. Tubs of a size to be used by one person at a time. Several months ago, however, friends invited us to spend some days with them at their condo. We had a bathroom all our own — with a shower. "You know," I told my wife after we'd been there about a week, "there may be something to this shower thing after all. It just might catch on."

So we came right home and engaged a man to put one in for us — our first. The house is old, and to get to the water pipes he had to cut through an adjoining wall, which dragged the project out a bit and somewhat increased the expense. He got it done, though. And it's a nice shower, if rather small.

Two persons probably could get in it, although it would be a tight fit. They could soap themselves up all right, but with the water pressure as low as it is it might take them as much as an hour to get rinsed off. Practically speaking, however, it's best suited for use by one at a time.

Let me say again that I respect other people's right to conduct themselves as they please. I'm often behind the times, and it might be that eventually — in the next life, if not in this one — I will come around to the idea of the tub for four.

At this moment, somewhere in one of the more cultured cities on the coasts, I suppose someone could be saying to a spouse, "Honey, we ought to do some entertaining. Let's invite a few neighbors over for drinks, dinner and a bath."

But for us, for the time being at least, our one little bitty shower will have to do — even if it does somewhat cramp our social life.

CALL HIM MR. LOUT

As may have come to your attention (but more likely has not), those of us who write for the newspaper have been issued a new manual intended to guide us in matters of style and usage. It goes without saying that this slender booklet, although very new, already has become the center of our thoughts and the largest single influence upon our waking lives.

Journalists, in case you do not know it, are ruled by habit. Even when speaking, we tend to see words with our mind's eye as they might appear on the printed page. No reporter worth the name, having once been given to understand the fine difference between a stone and a rock — the former can be picked up and thrown; the latter is too large — would confuse the two again.

That would be a piece of carelessness as inexcusable as the mistaking of a Trollope for a trollop, or a trollop for a truffle, or a truffle for a tart. In the same way that nations of people who live mainly on potatoes and turnips come physically to resemble those vegetables, we newspaper folk are powerfully shaped by our craft.

The new *Stylebook* — one word, italicized — counsels us on many subjects. One of those is the matter of courtesy titles, long an area of capriciousness and fearful indiscipline.

Henceforth, for regularity's sake, these titles will in almost every case be used. Males who have achieved the age of 18 years will, on second reference, be awarded the title of *Mister*. This will apply, democratically, to presidents of the republic, captains of industry and the humblest clerk alike.

Mister also will be used — and here, to be sure, a certain awkwardness intrudes — in speaking of international terrorists, extortionists, mob hit men, flashers, sodomists, mass murderers and, in spite of the possible damage to their careers, professional female impersonators.

An exception, is made for sports figures. Which means that a player who runs 90 yards from scrimmage in the waning seconds of the championship game must remain forever plain Smith. Whereas, if only he had run the same distance naked along a public street, getting a sunburn and frightening dogs, he could have been called Mr. Smith and gotten a measure of respect.

I leave to the resourcefulness of the editors the question of how to report the story of a peeping Tom named Tom Thomas. Would one describe him as the peeping Mr. Thomas? I cannot, for the life of me, figure out where the *Mister* goes.

In perfect evenhandedness, the rule mandates for women a choice between *Miss, Missus* or *Mizzzzz*, depending on their preference or the fact of their marital status. The debutante would surely be a *Miss*. But so would be the unwed murderess, the gangster's moll, the star of pornographic movies or the proprietress of a house for what my dictionary shyly describes as untidy ladies. Unless, of course, she favored being a *Mizzzzz*.

Such are the illogicalities of style.

The proper function of the writer, however, is not to cavil and complain, but rather to make use of the facts as they are given. The *Stylebook* is such a fact. And, in our daily lives as in our work, we are accommodating to it.

I have heard — or at least read — of couples who have passed through their entire marriages addressing one another as *Mister* and *Missus*. So evidently it can be managed, although for the children it seems to be harder at first.

Just last night, somewhere nearby in the neighborhood, an alarm went off and jerked us rudely from sleep. Unnerved and sitting bolt upright in the bed at that unnatural hour, listening to the siren whoop, I was assailed by awful worries.

What if the fleeing burglar sought refuge in my house? What if the noises of forced entry were heard at the door? What if he actually got inside?

What if I cried out for him to leave — and he didn't? Having used up that first permissible "Hey you!" how might I then address him in the second reference?

VI

THE LAND ABIDES

There's a fine directness in country dealings. The season mellows, the fallow fields begin to warm, and two men sit at a table with a pad of paper and cups of coffee between them.

Ahead lies the uncertain year, inscrutable in its possibilities for beneficence or ruin. There is no use trying to take weather into account, since it is a force of majestic caprice. Plans are made of things more sure.

The men speak the familiar names of fields: the mountain field, the cave meadow, the flood field, the front pasture, the middle field. It is a kind of shorthand, by which a map is unfolded in their minds. The history of each piece of ground is known, and its exact dimensions.

How can these tracts be used to good advantage? Is there some better service they might be put to than before? *What if ... ?*

The lined pad fills up with scribbled speculations, and with numbers in two columns. One column lists the costs. When added up, it tells exactly the sum at risk. The other suggests what the investment and the work might bring, but the forecast is undependable. It is a calculation skewed by hopes and remembered disappointments.

The trick, then, is to adjust that amount by a realistic factor that, on the one hand, will leave some reason to go forward, and, on the other, will prevent October and the price at harvest from entirely breaking your heart. And after that there is the question of how the risks and the rewards, if any, will be shared. It's crucial, this issue of *fairness*. For without it, all the rest will sour and surely fail.

Methodically these discussions proceed, from sum to sum, from field to field, until nothing is left on the table. For most of 20 years, now, I have taken part in these spring-time discussions — with a succession of men who have come and left, turning the earth of a tract of ground that, in the law's view, whatever that is worth, I've come to own.

I repeated the ceremony the other day, with a neighbor. He's a younger man than I, but well experienced in all these things. He's fair-dealing, as I mean to be, so the cooperation promises to go well. In a couple of hours we talked the whole year through, from now to winter.

As we were discussing, a spring storm rushed up from behind the trees and flung ahead of it a hard, cold rain and a spit of hail. Then, just as quickly, the sun came out again and returned a little warmth to the washed April afternoon.

After the neighbor left, I walked through the wet woods and up to the edge of one of the fields about which we'd just been speaking. The soil between the tan stalks of last year's crop was dark, with puddles shining. I tried to imagine what harvest of success or discouragement the land would yield me this time, but the field just lay there in silent, patient indifference.

Increasingly I have come to accept that the enterprises to which we attach such moment — those of us who gain and lose title to the land, and those who stir it to their profit or loss — really are of no particular importance.

We come. We scratch our careful numbers on a paper. We strive a while, wearing out our machines and eventually ourselves. We go. Then the seasons turn without us. The grateful land rests without us. Sooner than you'd suppose, there is no sure proof we ever were there at all. And it takes a fearful vanity to imagine otherwise.

LOOKING FOR LOOF LIRPA

It happened every year in the newsroom where I misspent my youth — a less professional place than the newspaper offices of today, but a lot more fun.

On a fine spring morning the newest, greenest reporter would stop at the assistant city editor's desk to look at the assignment sheet and learn how his day was to be occupied. He would find his name penciled in the left-hand column, beside what sounded like a good chance at a story — better, at any rate, than the obituaries and club notes on which beginners used to cut their teeth.

The Spanish bullfighter, Loof Lirpa, was stopping between planes on his way to an exhibition in Mexico City. The eager young newsman was instructed to meet the flight and interview the matador during his brief layover at the airport.

Accompanied by some grizzled veteran of a photographer, he would go there and station himself at the unloading gate. Out the people would come. Women and children. The portly. The dissolute and the infirm. But no one with the look or the carriage of somebody who made a practice of sauntering out with tight pants and a cape to face 1,000 pounds of horned fury.

The reporter's palms would go sweaty. It wouldn't do to bungle his first real assignment. "Better find him, kid," the photographer would growl.

Maybe he'd written down the flight wrong. There were other arrivals, from other cities. But which one? Our hero would rush in a panic then, first to one gate and then another — it was the old airport, the smaller one — searching in desperation for anyone who might pass for a bullfighter, any fellow with a swagger, a faintly bronzed skin or a little pigtail. "You aren't by any chance Loof Lirpa, are you?" he'd demand of perfect strangers. Veering away, they'd walk on past.

Defeated, finally — failed and sick at heart — he would give it up. "There's going to be hell to pay," the photographer would say reassuringly on the ride back to the office.

On legs heavy with despair, he would climb the stair to the newsroom — the place where he'd hoped to make a name for himself, but where his career was now wrecked almost at the start. Heads would turn as he slunk through the door. Fifty derisive pairs of eyes would be fixed upon him.

There would be a long silence. Then, from somewhere in the big room, a coarse guffaw was heard. Then others. Until the whole place rang with laughter that washed over him in his vast surprise. Even the editors would be laughing.

And he would understand that there was no malice in it. A prank, was all it was.

It happened to nearly every one of us, and always on

this same day of spring. Loof Lirpa, if you haven't guessed it already, is *April Fool* spelled backwards.

THE WEATHER REPORT

The spring comes haltingly, like a child already late to class or some old acquaintance arrived for a visit, unsure of the address and not quite certain of a welcome.

One day there's sun and the creak of insects as night comes on. The next there's a squall, with cold rain slanting and a voice of desolation keening on the wind. It's a season of confusion, this one. There's nothing to rely on.

A friend and I drove out the other morning on a serious errand. Sensibly, though, we took some fishing gear along in case the schedule should happen to change in a way altogether beyond our control. The early sky was clear and promising, the air sharp but still. Beyond the city, in the first sun, wild plum trees could be seen flowering along the field's edges, sudden white explosions against the dark winter-burn of woods.

We finished our business ahead of time and took lunch in the restaurant of a country town, perched with its courthouse and water tower and assorted steeples on a hill near the edge of a lake.

By now, a gray haze had blown up to cover the sky. The wind had risen to a raw gale, shaking trees, howling across the paving bricks of the town's square, churning the lake to slaty ranks of waves and sullen foam. No boat was out — only rafts of northing canvasback ducks afloat serenely on that tumult.

We were in our winter coats. Our fishing gear was absurdly out of season. So was the baseball game on the car radio. So were the plum trees and the yellow wash of forsythia and the clumps of feral daffodils gleaming wind-bent in the dooryards of houses occupied now by nothing except small histories and some farmer's bales of hay.

But enough description. You know exactly the sort of day it was, and perhaps even which particular day. Nothing much to remark about, though. About average for this time of year in this latitude. I got to thinking as we headed home, the car rocking and sometimes actually swerving a little in the blast, that maybe the glories of early spring have been somewhat overdone. We have it mainly on the testimony of poets, and poets, it is widely known, are not always the best reporters.

What distinguishes this season is its wild variety. It can contain — in the space of a week, a day or sometimes even a single hour — the most congenial weather and the most foul. And so, of all our seasons, it seems to me the one most reflective of our lives.

Surely summer is not a life — all lazy suffocation and prickly heat. And neither is winter. At least I've not known many lives that were all sleet and aching brittleness, without some accidental warmth of decency or hope. Autumn is flawless, and must be disqualified on that account. Its days proceed in mellow perfection. There is nothing about it you would amend. But fiercely as we insist that's what a life should be, it's not one that many of us would recognize from having lived it.

No, give me a spring every time — especially this

uncertain early part of it.

A day begun in comfort can end in raw despair. Or just as easily the other way around. There's something to be said for knowing the difference between the two. Flowers open and millers hatch and bugs crawl bravely out before the danger of a killing freeze is quite yet past. There are great gains in it, and fearful losses.

It is not really the ideal sort of weather but it is wonderfully familiar. It is the weather that our years have taught all of us to walk in. Or finally will.

A FOWL IDEA

The midlife crisis arrives at different times, in different ways. For me it has appeared late and strangely. I am overcome by an irrational desire to raise chickens.

No sooner will these words find print, I expect, than neighbors along my street will begin leafing frantically through the statute books and putting in calls for their lawyers. To city folk, the sound of a rooster at daybreak would rank only a little behind the *whoosh* of incoming ICBMs on the list of unwanted sounds.

They worry unnecessarily. Some follies you act out, and some you keep safely caged. A man like me might fall into a nest of showgirls or slip off to Fiji with a suitcase of company money. But he would never try anything as rash as keeping urban pullets.

The poultry lust came on me by pure accident. I was leafing through one of those slick-paper magazines for the country swells — the kind of publication that bears down hard on such cutting issues as the maintenance of split-rail fences, how to manage your compost heap, and the cultivation of decorative gourds.

There was a feature on the back yard chicken flock. That's what it said: the *back yard* flock. The evil spoke to me in that moment, like the serpent speaking to Eve from the tree. *"You have a back yard,"* it whispered — and the damage was done.

The pictures in the magazine were wonderful. Gaudy harem-masters, necks upstretched as they saluted the morning. Hens spewing fresh eggs. Clutches of chicks tumbling along after their mothers in happy parade across the grass. Anyone can keep fowl for decoration and amusement, the article said. And if the fun ever wears thin, you can eat your hobby.

I was remembering, then, the morning sounds in some of the places I have been. Not torpid backwaters, either, but major cities. Places like Amman, Jordan; Cairo; Lagos in Nigeria — the capitals of countries. Dawn comes, there, to a music finer than the hum of tires on asphalt, the *whop-whopping* of police helicopters and the screech of burglar alarms set off by cause or accident.

At the first pale streak of light across the rooftops one hears the strangled braying of asses from distant courtyards. Then the symphony of roosters starts up. You can stand at the window and watch the day come, reminded — in the same way we used to be reminded by the far-off hoot of a passing train — that the world is a vast and various place, and that life contains many possibilities.

What a pleasure it might be for the folks along my

street, and several other streets in all directions, to have their mornings announced by something more melodious than a bedside clock radio. It is a little gift of love I could give the neighborhood.

The magazine carried the address of a hatchery in Iowa that ships starter stock to anywhere in the country by overnight express. Today I wrote off for the free catalog, and that's as far as this foolishness has gone.

What can it hurt just to look at the catalog?

NOT IN *MY* BASEMENT

When the sky turns curdy green, the air grows breathless and the warning sirens sound, people acquainted with the violence of the midwestern spring know what they are supposed to do. They are supposed to go to the basement.

But you have not seen my basement. If going down there is the price of survival, the price is too high. I am prepared to cower in the bathtub with my family pressed close around me. Or to take shelter under table or bed. Or to go outside and lie in the road ditch while the maelstrom whirls over and past.

Maybe these precautions will save me and maybe not. In any case, I will not go to the basement.

For one thing, the sirens may not have anything at all to do with the weather. It could be that the look of the sky is a pure coincidence, and that the real reason for the sirens is that a Russian ballistic missile is coming at me

across the Arctic circle. If so, the advantage of the basement over the bathtub does not seem particularly significant.

I do not mean to give the impression of raw bravado. I
am as afraid of violent storms as anyone. It is just that I am
somewhat more afraid of the basement. It has what I imagine to be the feel of a Ugandan prison. The walls sweat.
The drains do not drain. Small, quick things can be seen
— or sensed — to move in the shadows among the boxes,
the old furniture, the stacked and mounded residue of our
lives and all the lives before us in the house.

The cats go down in the basement. The jungle feel of
the place appeals to them. But they spend their time
prowling the overhead pipes and ductwork, safe above the
yeasty pools and moist ruin of the floor. I am heavier than
the cats and not as nimble. There is no room for me there
on the pipes.

I have a nightmare. It is that sometime we will be having a party and it will be spring and at some point during
the evening — between the chicken Kiev, say, and the
bananas Foster — the sky will get that look and the sirens
will begin and our guests will say, *"Well, let's all go to the
basement."*

I will try to temporize. There is no use to panic, I will
tell them. Maybe it is not a cyclone. Maybe it is only the
start of World War III. But they will insist. *"To the basement!"* they will cry. Faced, then, with the prospect of a
nasty scene, possibly even panic and violence and later
threats of litigation, I will have no choice but to allow the
guests to go down and crawl around on the pipes with the
cats.

If the alarm is for a storm, I will have suffered, at a minimum, a social calamity of the first order. If it is for missiles, I will have shamed myself to no point.

Either way, the hope of recovery will be slight.

So What's a Weed?

Violets have claimed at least the front quarter of the lawn, where sunlight falls. And Creeping Charlie, an aggressive vining plant, has taken most of the rest.

A scandal our lawn may be, by the standards of the governing homeowners' association. But treading out barefoot today into the dew-dampness of an early spring morning, I understood finally that I would have it no other way. If it is scandalous, at least it's a scandal of sweet flowering. And only in this short moment of a season is the gift of beauty so freely given.

I picked a little bunch of wild blossoms and brought them in, then had a devil of a time finding anything small enough for a vase. An empty pill container finally served to hold them, and they're on the table now beside me where they can be examined more closely.

The violets are of three distinct varieties. The flowers of all have five petals, but their colors are different. One is of that rich shade commonly spoken of — how else? — as *violet,* with just a bit of white at the throat. A second kind is lighter, the petals white at the margins, but delicately veined with purple, the veining growing darker toward the center. The third sort is practically all white, with only the least hint of any other color.

Oddly, while all three variants are everywhere represented, one kind or another appears to dominate in various sectors of the yard. What accounts for that I can't say — whether it's pure accident, or possibly some slight difference in microclimate between locations only a dozen feet apart.

The Creeping Charlie, too, is magnificent this time of year. Its flowers are very small — smaller than a single petal of the violet — and trumpet shaped. The color is a periwinkle blue, with white and maroon markings deep in the trumpet's bell. I'd never really taken time to notice them before. But I have to say they contribute subtly by creating a kind of faint blue background against which the bolder colors of the violets show to fine advantage.

Here and there, through this low carpet of blossoms, occasional patches of grass can be seen. But they appear to be limited in extent and well controlled, and do not too much detract from the larger effect.

As nearly as I can tell by looking from the window, ours is the only lawn on the block so richly decorated. In both directions, as far as one can see, there's only an unrelieved sameness of green. I suppose one day a delegation will appear at the door to report that Creeping Charlie and violets have begun to infect neighboring yards, and that we are suspected of being the source of the contagion. "You're harboring weeds," they'll say.

"What's a weed?" I'll reply. *"A plant whose virtues have not yet been discovered."*

"Who said that?"

"Emerson did."

"Well, you mustn't neglect your grounds the way you have. It's against the rules."

"Whoso would be a man must be a non-conformist," I'll tell them.

"More Emerson?"

"Who else?"

"We're warning you," the spokesman will say. "It can't go another summer like this."

"Do what we can," I'll tell them, *"summer will have its flies. If we walk in the woods, we must feed mosquitoes."*

"What's that supposed to mean?"

"I don't know, but it has a nice ring."

By one measure, the prolific flowering of our yard is a nuisance that $25 worth of herbicide could set right. To our eye, it is a celebration.

SONGS OF TOADS

Journalism is a hasty art.

If there were time, I would like to research extensively the question of toads, because I think, as with anything that lives and lusts and perishes, there must be a good deal about them worth knowing. What I have, instead, is only the product of an hour's casual observation.

We were beside a pond in one of the cow pastures, my daughter and I. The afternoon breeze had hushed. The evening was coming softly on.

A few moments before, a family of a dozen geese had crested a woodline and passed low overhead on their way to the night's resting place. In the great stillness, the rush of their wingbeats could be clearly heard. Together we watched the sun fall, and the sky across the field richen with a blend of peach and darkest blue. It was a good time to be anywhere, especially with someone who's a friend.

Suddenly, from the far side of the pond, an electronic trill was heard. A moment later, from another quarter of the shore, an answer was hurled back. All around the perimeter, then, there rose a gathering chorus, growing in number of voices, intensifying in shrillness. Until we were wrapped entirely in a din of creaking and screaming so vast that it seemed to fill the whole visible universe and resonate inside the head. Each voice was slightly different in tone. Each song distinct in its cadence or duration. Plainly, though, the singers were of the same race of creature.

Singling one voice out from the others, my daughter followed the racket to its source. Its author was a toad. A surprisingly small toad, an inch of him at most, grayish-brown on top, perched at the pond's edge. We knelt to see him better in the poor light, and he was undisturbed by our being there. He had other things to think about, and work to do.

As we bent close, he inflated his throat to perhaps half the size of his whole body, and then shot out a burst of sound that lasted 10 seconds or maybe 15. Unless we'd seen it, we'd never have believed a beast that small capable of so terrific a howl. If human beings could emit a cry of such dimension proportionate to our size, it would be a nightmare weapon able to blow down buildings and knock airplanes from the sky.

We watched him, amazed, through several repetitions

of his feat, which he seemed to take pretty much for granted. And all around the little pond were dozens, or possibly hundreds, of other virtuosos like himself. I say *himself,* although for all I know the singers may have been *herselves.* Or it could be that, with toads, both genders sing.

You see, there's the handicap of never having time to look into things properly.

If I had to guess, I'd say their performance had something to do with the season of the year and the time of reproduction. Probably they were singing to charm another toad. But why would that be necessary, considering the great multitude of them around the pond and the fact that toads, in any case, have only other toads to go to?

On the other hand, if their songs were different, mightn't their purposes be different too? Maybe some of them were crying out cautionary arias about the raccoon that comes at night or the heron with his skewering beak. Maybe some were singing for the pure joy of being toads on such an evening.

Maybe some had been told they had nice voices.

We watched until it was too dark to see them any more, and we couldn't know.

But toads know.

FORGET I MENTIONED IT

I had a friend who labored 20 years or more in this business, writing diligently, stylishly, on a subject he considered to be of serious consequence. Hardly anyone ever mentioned the work he was about.

Then, to make some pocket change or help pay for a trip he'd taken, he dashed out a hasty piece of froth — a humorous, inconsequential little ditty about getting fitted for a custom-made suit by a gentleman's tailor in London.

The applause was thunderous. People couldn't say enough nice things about the story — people who'd never bothered to so much as mention his regular writing. After a while, he got the feeling his whole identity had been taken over by that bit of nonsense tossed off almost without a thought. It broke his heart. Not so long afterward, he gave up writing. And a while after that, he got out of newspapering altogether

Well, I can better understand now how he felt. It happened after a recent piece I wrote about a sudden, unaccountable desire to keep backyard chickens.

Neighbors passing on the block — people I wasn't sure knew I was regularly employed — have stopped to inquire which day my flock would be arriving. An acquaintance called to let me know she had some exotic chicks coming by express freight, and would be glad to share her order.

A man on the next street wrote to say that, if I got a rooster, he hoped it would be a loud one. All the way from Ohio came a kind reader's invitation to bring an entry for the late-May International Chicken Flying Meet, to be held on the edge of a cliff in Gallia County, with a $1,000 prize for the longest flight exceeding the established record of 302 feet 8 inches, set 10 years ago by a bantam named Lola B. from West Virginia.

Everywhere I go, now, the subject seems to come up. A colleague even asked the other day if I'd finished building my coop. (For the record, I haven't even begun.) If it can destroy a career to become the Saville Row Suit Man, what hope can there be for the Chicken Columnist?

One reader's letter, though, I have to share verbatim. It clearly came from a woman of some experience. Said she:

Recently you wrote of your impulse to acquire chickens. Before you do something that may result in unhappiness and disillusionment, consider my experience. I grew up on a small farm and loved everything about it but the chickens. They are subject to infestations of mites so that, when sent to gather the eggs, I would return not only with eggs but covered with crawling mites from the walls and door of the chicken house.

When it rains, a hen with chicks will seek a spot under a downspout where the water will drown her chicks unless rescued . . . A chicken has intelligence just above that of a grub worm. A rooster, acquired for breeding purposes, came through the air, beak and spurs flashing, and gouged a hole in the back of my little sister's head. She could not go outdoors thereafter until he was executed. When the hen was seen eating

a snake head-first, it dulled the appetite we all
had for fried chicken. Would you want to put up
with all this just to hear the crow of a rooster at
dawn?

Sincerely,

Josephine Dee

No indeed, Miss Dee, I certainly would not!

So much for the brief fame this thing has gotten me.
The subject of chickens is permanently closed.

SECRETS OF THE GARAGE

In the 21 years I shared my parents' home, my father
never once cleaned out the garage.

He had many virtues. He was a faithful husband, a lov-
ing parent, loyal to his friends and a congenial neighbor to
other men along the block. I believe he smoked a cigarette
once, in the basement, just to see if there might be any
pleasure in it. There wasn't, and he gave it up after one.
The garage was his single flaw.

It was a small garage, built when cars also were small.
When vehicles got longer, he had to extend the structure
by two feet to the rear, but he managed to accomplish that
without cleaning the place out. The clutter was all but
impenetrable. My mother refused ever to enter there, and
I was afraid to. If he thought something he needed might
be somewhere in the tangle of the lightless interior, he had
to back the car out to look for it.

It is tragic how the generations repeat.

My wife and I have lived in this house of ours the greater part of our married life and raised our family between its walls. Our garage is larger than my father's was, designed for two cars. It's filled up just the same though, and for as long as I remember I've had to park on the drive.

A week or so ago I decided, on impulse, that after 30 years it might be about time to tidy the place up a bit. So I put on grubby clothes, screwed up my nerve and raised the door. There used to be an electric door lifter, but it broke, or we threw away the clicker when it seemed unlikely we'd ever want in there again. The interior was dank as a pharaoh's tomb. Spiders' webs hung like a veil, beaded with the crisp husks of bugs sucked dry and forgotten. Leaves of long-ago seasons rotted underfoot.

In the half-light through the crusted panes, the variety of the artifacts was astounding:

A broken Flexible Flyer sled; four bicycles, two of adult size and two smaller; a shelf of paints gone dry in the can, and jars of clear fluids whose nature and purpose could not be guessed; a bag of concrete solidified in the sack; a car tire and the rim for a different tire; coils of rope; a moist tangle of plastic sheeting.

And more: a baby bed and mattress; two tables and eight chairs from the daughters' college years; cartons of flatware and dishes; sheaves of books and papers, chewed at the edges; an ancient meat smoker, somehow still dripping grease; an aquarium in which the doomed had gasped their last; a plastic box whose latch the cats had solved to prey on the pet lizard.

And still more: various crates and boxes; two little wagons, one a Radio Super, the other a Rex Pal; a yellow desk and gray rolling chair; a plant stand; a Round Oak wood heating stove; a bag of fertilizer split and spilling; gasoline cans, empty; a push-type lawn mower; garden tools all rusted and broken.

Also rolled carpets; skis; 13 suitcases; two hubcaps; a draftsman's table; a broken bureau; a futon frame; a wicker chest; four ladders; an enormous screen door; a quantity of chicken wire; several wooden pallets; and a lifetime supply of anti-freeze.

And that was only the topmost layer.

I could spy a gleam of red from farther down, so I dragged more detritus aside, gave a little cry and rushed inside the house. "You'll never guess what I found," I told my wife.

"A raccoon?"

"No, a *Volkswagen!*"

"You're kidding. The red one?"

"Right," I said. "I'd forgotten it was still around here somewhere."

It was a '71 bug, bought used — a daughter's first car. "How long has it been?" she asked.

"Eleven years," I said. "And can you believe there's still air in the tires?"

Which only goes to show it pays to clean the garage at least once in a lifetime, whether it needs it or not.

ON THE BROOKLYN HILL

I haven't altogether forgotten being young. The feelings of it still come, but they are farther between.

Waking beside an open window in the freshness of October morning, it's possible sometimes to believe that six decades of injuries have been healed by sleep. Or standing alone after dark out on the lawn I hear, from across some great distance, the hooting of a train. And the way to everywhere seems open again.

A shudder passes through me. Then the moment's gone.

One golden afternoon not long ago, halted at a traffic light, I watched a boy on a skateboard zip through the crosswalk. The curbs, negotiated with two nimble little hops, hardly even slowed him.

He was 16 or maybe 17 years old — a hound-thin rail of a lad, wearing blue jeans, shirttail flying in the wind, a baseball cap turned backward on his head. The rush hour had just begun, and we in our cars were caught in the traffic's erratic flow. By the time the signal changed, the boy, with effortless flicks of the propelling foot, had flashed away out of sight.

And I remembered how easy it used to be — how little distance meant. My friend from the earliest times lived five blocks away — uphill going there, downhill coming home. It was just a fine run, not quite enough to make the breath come hard.

The homeward trip, at supper hour in the cool of the

autumn turning, was the best. Brooklyn Avenue fell away in a long even slant ahead. You didn't so much run that hill as simply release your legs in an abandonment of free fall. No ankle ever turned. No stitch ever knifed at the side. Such possibilities never even crossed the mind. All the known houses flashed past in a windy blur in the blue dusk. It was the nearest thing to pure, unaided flight I ever knew until, in middle age, I learned to ski.

That's how I remembered it. But could youth really have been that good?

I followed the traffic on to my turn-off that recent day. And then, needing to go out on some later errand, was passing along a street in a far quarter of the city when who should be seen but that same boy — no mistaking him — still swooping and gliding like a hawk in the air currents, shirt flying, eyes squinty with the pleasure of being a creature in his prime.

How many miles had he covered? Fifteen, maybe. But what difference did it make? Why would he notice? *Yes,* I thought then, *memory doesn't lie. Youth really was that fine!*

And for just that instant — a moment so swift and delicate it couldn't be held — I was on the Brooklyn hill again, with the year changing and everyone I cared about still alive, almost airborne in the glad rush toward tomorrow, with no cracks in the sidewalk to catch a shoe.

WE ARE FAMILY ENOUGH

The kitchen drawer in which Scoop's things are kept is too high for him to reach. By standing atop a box, however, and stretching to his full height, he was able to open the drawer and select his favorite toy, the fuzzy orange ball.

This accomplishment, and the obvious act of reasoning that directed it, would not have been particularly noteworthy in a child — even a small and fairly limited child. But Scoop isn't a child. He's a cat, a black one, born under a newspaperman's bed and heir to all the unfortunate habits of poking and prying that go with the journalist's trade.

While Scoop was opening the drawer and rifling through its contents, the white cat, Teddy, was busy in what my wife calls his office.

This "office" is a cabinet in the breakfast room, where towels, napkins, place mats and folded sheets are kept. The sheets are for covering car seats while transporting furred members of the household to their various appointments. The cabinet's doors latch when closed, but Teddy has solved the latch.

Each day, faithful as any clerk punching the clock, he opens his office and drags out the sheets. His purpose in doing it is not obvious, but he would not dream of letting a day go by without tending to this important work.

And then there is the new kitten — yes, *another one!* — who remains unnamed. That's because he is a transient, bound at month's end for a more cosmopolitan life. He'll be a New Yorker, and his business there will be to entertain and console a young woman, our daughter, filling as best he can the empty place left by the loss of gentle Albert, the last of the three who'd shared her college years.

But until she comes to claim him, he lodges with us.

He rests handily on one open palm, and weighs something over a pound, maybe nearer two. The pups, who also are citizens here, are upwards of 40 pounds apiece. They're bird dogs. But on occasion have been squirrel dogs, even rabbit dogs. I cannot imagine them ever deliberately being cat dogs, but in a moment of confusion or excitement, something regrettable might happen.

So we isolated the new one in a room of his own. He objected, shoving objects under the crack of the door to petition for freedom. When released, quite unmindful of his own smallness, he strode directly to the nearest of the dogs and sniffed the various parts of him, frightening the great hunter almost witless.

The pups take their meals in the kitchen, and it is an important moment of their day. I fill the bowls, then retire to the table with the newspaper and my first coffee. The cats, respecting the ceremony of it, mostly keep their distance.

Yesterday morning, though, hearing a whine, I looked up to see the orange dog, Pete, who'd moved a couple of feet back from the bowl, wearing an expression of profound sorrow as he observed that mite of a kitten shoulder-deep in his breakfast.

Behind me, I could hear Teddy in his office, dragging out sheets. Scoop was up on his box, feeling with one arm over the rim of the drawer.

Now the smallest one of all was trying to starve the dogs.

And in that somber early hour it was revealed clearly to me, if I'd ever doubted it, that any hope of order in this crowded life of ours had long ago been lost.

MY MONEY'S WORTH

Maybe I am prisoner of an archaic thrift, but I always like to feel that I have gotten the full use out of my property.

My automobile, for example, has 150,000 miles on its odometer. When I drive it to weddings, or am invited to parties a bit above my social station, I am careful to park my machine around a corner or, if possible, on the next street. But as long as it starts most mornings and can be made to go forward and backward on command, it serves as well as any car I would be apt to get by taking a second mortgage on the house and selling my daughters into white slavery.

This prudence governs small matters as well as large.

The other day, while walking in a gentle rain, my attention was drawn to a wetness on my right foot. I looked down, and noticed that my shoe had broken in half. It had been a quality shoe — still was, except for this one imperfection. I bought that pair and another at a two-for-one sale eight, maybe 10 years ago. They didn't have two pairs in my size, so I took a pair a half-size too small and wore those out first so I would have comfort to look forward to.

When I say the shoe had broken in half, I don't mean
completely in half. Just across the top, where the foot bends.
The rest of it was perfectly all right. The two halves still
were attached to the sole which, along with the heel, had
been replaced no more than two years ago. I stood a
moment in the rain, considering what further good I
might get out of those shoes, possibly as sandals.

But that was for the future. The immediate problem
was that I had to go to the office and after that to a luncheon at a nice place, and you cannot park your shoes on the
next street without being thought eccentric. So I got in my
car, which started one more time, and drove to an outlet I
know where the merchandise smells of smoke and the proprietor's heart leaps up every time he hears a fire truck
pass.

Would you believe that you still can get a serviceable
pair of shoes for about $100? Now I'm not talking tassels
and gold buckles and zippers up the side. Just something
no-nonsense and sturdy. But it's nice to know that, even
after 40-some years of inflation, it is possible to buy a pair
of shoes for only twice what I paid for my first car.

I asked the salesman what kind of price he might be
able to make on two pairs. He thought it over and said
$200. It was attractive, but I passed it up. I wouldn't lay out
that kind of money for a second pair of shoes, even in the
right size, without first getting a thorough physical
checkup.

At the luncheon nobody said anything about my shoes,
which was disappointing. You would like to get an immediate return on your investment. I kept crossing my legs so
the new soles would show, but the people I was with were

inattentive or possibly unimpressed.

At the theater that night it was different, though. "There you are," a friend said, "in your new brown suit."

Actually, the suit was several years old and was the result of another two-for-one sale. It's just that I hadn't worn it before. The truth is I hate brown suits — on me, that is. On other people they're fine. I found a gray pin-stripe one that suited me and said I would take two of those. "You can't get two suits exactly alike," my wife told me.

"Why not?" I said.

"How will anyone ever know you have a second suit?"

"OK," I said. "The brown one, then." And I hung it in the closet where it stayed until, by pure coincidence, I happened to be wearing it for the first time on the same day my shoe broke in half. "Do you notice anything else?" I asked my friend at the theater, crossing and uncrossing my legs, showing my soles.

"Your right sock looks wet."

"Yes," I said sadly. "It's been a day of transition."

VII

HARD BEGINNINGS

One spring it was a coyote that whelped under my cabin floor. Other springs a fox brought off her kits there.

Forty years ago, in a hard spell of winter, a passing tire struck down a beagle mama a short way down my country road and scattered her orphaned pups across those wooded hills. Two of them made a nest beside a log at the back of the cabin clearing and tried to find a living baying after rabbits in the night. Eventually those two joined me indoors beside the stove, and we spent the next 14 years together.

It has always pleased me, somehow, that so many creatures needing shelter have found their way to that humble place at the woods' edge.

This year it is a black, short-legged dog with pricked ears, friendly eyes and no identifiable — or even guessable — ancestry. I've no idea where she came from, though possibly from the house of the new people on the far side of the road. She looks well-enough nourished, but clearly no provision was made for the birthing, so she'd had to find a place.

All night I heard her little ones mewing and scuffling under the cabin floor, directly below my bed. And in the morning, slipping quietly onto the porch and peering around a corner, I finally saw them. There were two: fuzzy bundles of cinnamon-colored fur, with broad little faces and black markings — the mother's gift — around their eyes and muzzles. I supposed she'd gone off to wherever someone had set out a pan of food, because the pups sat pressed close together, giving impatient little yips, wanting her to hurry back with those faucets of life.

I stepped outside, then, and instantly those two were gone, back through the hole between the ground and the cabin's bottom log — back to the dark and safety of the den. Soon, though, curiosity overcame them. One nose was thrust out, then the other. Then both ventured forth. Plainly they knew nothing of people, and no hand had ever touched them. Nor would mine.

I spoke softly and, kneeling, waited a bit. One of them, the smaller, wanted to come — took a couple of timid steps forward but could advance no farther. The danger was too great. When I stood, both disappeared into their hole again and stayed there until most of an hour later, when I noticed from my window that the mother had come back. She let them nurse. And afterward, while she stood watch, they tumbled in the grass outside their den, happy under the warm sun of another perfect day.

Absorbed in their play, they paid no attention when I stepped outside again. The mother came to me, cautious at first, then eagerly. She seemed glad to be spoken to and stroked. It must be a lonely business to bear your young unattended in the dark of a borrowed place. Were there just the two, or did only two survive?

There cannot be much future for cur pups who enter the world as unnoticed accidents in a country neighborhood. Those two can imagine nothing of what waits. For a bit longer, they will not feel the sting of curdom, will not know they are unwanted. For now, life is sweet perfection — or would be if that two-legged creature would not come trespassing, tromping about heavily on the boards above.

That afternoon I drove back to the city. The gate is closed now, the cabin locked and silent, that little piece of property entirely theirs again. And I don't begrudge their use of it. Their need is greater than my own. And for them, as for so many newborns of the world, childhood lasts hardly a moment.

IMAGINING OTHER PLACES

Green as England the country lies, after a spring that somehow lost its way. First the rains wouldn't come at all, and wildfires scoured the parched fields. Then, when the rains did begin, they refused to stop.

There was snow in April, and hail in May. A late frost ruined the season's flowering. One week you needed the furnace to take the edge off the morning's chill. The next week the temperature went to 90, and people were telephoning in a panic to get their air conditioners tuned.

So now it's summer ahead of time, and the true misery commences. There are good things to be said about the midlands. But we don't live here for the weather.

I'm remembering again a summer party we gave once at the farm. As I imagined it, we would be like figures in a painting by Monet — the women in airy skirts and wide-brimmed hats, the men all handsome in blazers and boating pants. We would drink crisp chilled wine and eat ice cream with wild berries over it. The conversation would be brilliant at a minimum.

That was how I saw it.

But the thermometer at midday said 107. The wine went flat, the berries soured, the ice cream turned to soup. And the mood of the guests was sullen. One woman passed the whole afternoon driving around the country roads with the car air conditioner blowing on high. The others, hammered by the heat, sat glumly on folding chairs around the tub of decaying refreshments. "We'll be all right," said one of them, "if nobody talks."

Then they all went back to the city to treat their chigger bites and pull off ticks.

After that we held no more parties at the farm.

What we do instead, now, is spend this season thinking of other places we would rather be. One of them is in the mountains. There's a place I know where a little stream runs down across a flowery meadow and bends to make a pool beside a rock. Even in the deep of summer it's so cold at the daybreak hour that the wet fly line in your hand can make the fingers ache.

The only trouble is that getting there means driving west across the naked plains, the sun white-hot and swollen four times its normal size. And if the ladies in your party insist on leaving the highway to visit the outlet mall that lurks there in the middle of Kansas, it's probable you'll die.

Paris is another of those places. The Paris summer of the year we spent there was wonderfully cool — two blankets in July — and I recall that like a gift. But that was a long time ago, before the U.S. dollar turned frail against the franc. Paris would be less wonderful, I expect, for an American family sleeping on benches in the Tuileries and eating from the bins out back of restaurants remembered fondly.

The other place that comes to mind — to which no handicaps attach — is in the far north of Minnesota, up where eagles turn and the loons cry and the roads are only sand ribbons running between stands of towering pines. It's easily gotten to in one long day, or a day and a half at most. With every mile northward, you can feel the heat lessen. The light changes, and shadows become sharp and dark.

It will not be many days, now, before the black mallards begin bringing off their hatches in the reeds at the lake's edge. At night, great fish rising will send silver circles across the moonlit water. And the sky will be a chilly sea of stars.

More summers than I can count we've fled there to escape the stifle. I suppose it's where we'll go again. In fact, I'm already there in my mind. But August will be the earliest chance, and August is an eternity away, with only suffering from now until then.

May seems much too early to have to start counting the days.

CHANCES ARE . . .

Lives are composed of sequential accidents. Sometimes planning plays hardly any part.

By accident, the people who moved as renters into the house on the far side of my country lane had a dog.

By chance — most assuredly by chance — that dog, a female Australian shepherd mix, was bred by some wandering cad of the neighborhood, a gigolo of unknown provenance.

Somewhat less accidentally, I suspect, she denned her new pups under my cabin floor.

When my wife and I were there one recent day, the mother dog, nudged her two woolly brown youngsters forward with her nose so they could be touched.

The consequence of these random occurrences is that the two pups no longer make their home under the cabin, 100 miles from here. Instead, they are in the dog pen about 15 feet from our bedroom window. And that much, at least, is deliberate. The ride back from the country must have been a terror. After which, in two days at the veterinarian's, they suffered all sorts of alarming ministrations — were stuck with needles, dewormed, deticked, bathed, and even had their toenails trimmed.

All gussied up and sanitized, they're with us now. And I have to say they're about the softest little creatures I ever touched. Yesterday we had them on the lawn, and children came from across the street to inspect the livestock. There's something miraculous in the chemistry between children and very young animals. In just part of an hour, all timidity was gone and the pups had been wholly socialized.

They're temporary lodgers only. The resident Brittanys, Pete and Bear, are decent sports, and have always preferred the freedom of the yard to confinement in the wire run. But now that the pen is occupied by others, its desirability has been much enhanced. From their manner I can tell they're wondering if they'll get it back.

Last night, the puppies' first in these new surroundings, loneliness or darkness overcame them and they set up a keening that I heard through the window at the edge of sleep. By yet one more accident — a happy one — the night was warm, almost like summer, so the neighbors on that side had their windows closed and their air conditioner running.

Last week I had a letter from a reader who said he would be interested in having one of the pups. He's to come today to look at them, and we're hoping he'll decide they oughtn't to be separated, and will want to take them both.

I simply cannot write about this again. To borrow one of psychobabble's favorite terms, readers want *closure*. I want closure. The neighbors need closure, and the editors demand it.

Above all, the pups need closure.

I hope, when he comes this morning, the man brings some closure with him.

A postscript: The man and his son showed up as promised, with their older dog, Rocky, and tried to pick between the two. They couldn't, though — and so decided the brothers could spend their lives together, after all. Such goodness, if there were enough to go around, might change the world.

CLEARED FOR TAKE-OFF

There are a lot of people complaining about getting laid off from their jobs at the casino, but one fellow I ran into swore it was the best thing that ever happened to him. "I learned a lot there," he said. "And now I've gone in business for myself."

"That's terrific. What kind of business?"

"I've started an airline," he said. And he drove me out to see his first plane.

We turned off a gravel road and into a farm field just outside the city limits, where he stopped the car. In the middle of the field was a squatty cement block building. "Well," I said, "where's the plane?"

"You're looking at it."

"What I'm looking at is a hog house."

"That's my plane," he said. "I've got folding chairs inside."

"It'll never fly."

"That's a technicality," he said. "Do you think those things they call *riverboats* will ever float? But they sell cruises on them, don't they?"

I had to admit he had me there. "In fact," he said, "I'm already booking flights."

"Flights to where?"

"Nowhere. It's sort of like those cruises. You get on and get off, and you haven't been anywhere."

"I'd hate to be in your shoes when the state finds out," I told him.

"No problem. I'm already licensed. All they wanted to talk about was their percentage. There's only one issue."

"What's that?"

"The fare limit. They put a $500 limit on the tickets I can sell. And I say that's unfair. If I can persuade somebody to pay a couple of grand to sit in a hog house, what business is that of the bureaucrats? Isn't that how free enterprise works?"

"A lot of the time, yes. But won't your porkers — I mean your passengers — complain?"

"What's to complain about? A virtual flight or a virtual cruise — there's no difference. Besides, we're going to be upgrading our service. By next week we'll have snacks, soft drinks and in-flight movies. Maybe even slot machines."

"Slots would help."

"And right now I'm negotiating for a second plane. It's a chicken coop on a farm a couple of miles south. It's old, but it's solid as a 707."

"I'll have to hand it to you," I told him. "It's a very original venture."

"There'll be imitators," he said. "You know how it's been with the boats. Sooner or later the bubble bursts. But we're in on the ground floor."

We got back in the car and headed back into town. "Do you plan to go public?" I asked him.

"Maybe sometime," he said. "Right now we're watching cash flow, trying not to grow the company too fast."

As I was getting out, he handed me an envelope. "Just a little thank-you for your time and your interest," he said.

Inside the envelope was my frequent-flier card.

THE SOUND OF MUSIC

We are visiting our New York daughter, and it is half-past 3 o'clock in the morning. In the apartment directly below, occupied by three Argentine rock musicians, the party still is going hard.

I sit on the edge of the bed, because if I lie down the *ka-whunk* of the electric bass comes up through the floor, into the legs of the bed and through the pillow to my ear. It's like being at the party, but with nothing to drink. So I sit on the bed and look through the window at the shine of a streetlight along the empty Brooklyn street and am toying with the idea of committing a terrorist act.

From time to time, the daughter's black cat, Valentine, comes to stand in the bedroom door and look at me sitting on the bed. Valentine rarely permits himself to be seen by day. He lives under the futon or in the springs of the bed. When he is feeling exceptionally nervous he goes behind the kitchen stove and hides somewhere in the workings of the gas oven.

New York can get you crazy that way.

The daughter hasn't used the stove in months for fear of incinerating the cat. So there's nothing in the refrigerator. She gets carry-out from the deli instead, or cooks in the microwave. But the kitchen is small. The only place to put the microwave is on top of the empty refrigerator, and there are only so many dishes one can prepare while cooking at a level two feet above one's head.

Probably if she ate in, instead of spending a fortune on carry-out, she would be able to afford a place with a modern stove that a cat couldn't get inside, and quiet neighbors on the next floor down. But now, in order to eat in, she'd have to risk cooking Valentine, so it is a vicious circle.

At 4 o'clock the party moves from the first floor of the building into the street, which I take for a sign that the affair may be winding down. As nearly as I can tell, they have been playing the same song — at least the beat is the same — for six and a half hours without interruption.

That was last night.

Today, my wife and daughter, who slept through the party, were rested and refreshed. Valentine and I are frazzled. If there were room for me inside the stove, I would go in there with him.

We took a bus and a train into Manhattan for breakfast, then spent a couple of hours at a museum, had a light lunch in the museum cafeteria, and stopped to watch the dogs and their owners at one of the fenced dog walks New Yorkers have in their public parks.

It was getting well on in the day when we came back to Brooklyn.

Hasidic men, perspiring in fur hats and black frock coats on a day in the 80s, were passing self-contained and mysterious along the sidewalks of the neighborhood.

And on the stoop outside the apartment on the building's bottom floor the Argentine musicians — fresh as new daisies — were just then having their breakfast. Orange juice and toast, in the middle of afternoon. "They're students at Juilliard," said our daughter.

"You don't say."

They looked like nice enough young men, but I was uninterested in their educational careers. It was their plans for later that worried me. I am not a swinging New Yorker. I am a man of regular habits, with a tidy little life, and there's no telling what could happen if I have to spend another night sitting on the edge of the bed.

Sure enough, just as I lay down, I heard a preliminary *ka-whunk* of the electric bass warming up. "We're in for it," I told Valentine the cat — wherever he happened to be.

But it was a false alarm. Somebody had knocked over a trash can down on the street.

New York can get you crazy that way.

CHUMPS AND HUZEES PROTEST

News out of Italy that scientists now are able to combine the genetic material of a human being with a chimpanzee and create a hybrid creature — known perhaps as a *chump* or a *huzee* — is deeply alarming.

The world does not need more newspaper columnists.

So far, apparently, these monstrous experiments have not been allowed to run their full course. That is, no living product of this tampering has yet been loosed upon the world. But the governing principle of science is anything that can be done *will* be done. So I am willing to bet that it will not be many years before chumps and huzees are everywhere around us.

Apart from journalism, this race of subhumans could be useful in many ways, some scientists say. Groups of them, for example, could be trained to perform tedious and unrewarding tasks in factories. They would work, literally, for peanuts. Human beings would be liberated from the assembly line, freed to perform tedious and unrewarding tasks in offices and elsewhere.

Huzees and chumps also would be a source of anatomical replacement parts. They could be maintained on farms, jogging, playing racquetball, studying aerobic dance. Booze and tobacco would be withheld. So that when opportunity called — the opportunity to be opened and eviscerated — their vital organs would be of the highest quality.

Humans would live forever. Chumps and huzees, being good citizens, would not ask what the country could give them, but what they could give the country. The answer would be hearts, livers, kidneys, lungs and so forth.

The problem is that, being half human, these handy creatures would one day get independent notions. It's an outrageous tendency, which is apt to appear in anyone with even the least trace of humanity. In time, they would learn to speak, perhaps even in a primitive way to write. Their vocabulary would be limited, but it would suffice for dealings among themselves.

They would consider and discuss. They would learn to chip stones into sharpened blades. Sooner or later, one supposes, they would organize in groups to demand change. Preposterous, you say? But a horse will try to throw a brutal rider. Even a dog, beaten repeatedly without cause, can learn to bite its master's hand. And these new creatures, remember, have the taint of us in them.

I would not want to be a keeper at the organ farm on the day the inmates figured out why no chump or huzee who went to the doctor ever came back. And I would not like to have to explain to a child the world that pure science, ungoverned by morality, might be able to make.

HOPE KEEPS YOU YOUNG

Now that I can't smoke, have to write on a computer and hardly know a soul in the room, about the only reason for hanging around the newspaper office is on the chance of receiving a little sexual harassment.

You hear all the time about sexual harassment in the workplace. Joe says to Hortense that he thinks she's swell-looking. Before he knows it, Joe's wearing leg irons in a holding tank with Colombian drug dealers, waiting to be put up as Exhibit A in a million-dollar suit against the company.

If Joe had told Hortense he thought she was a porker, that would have been fine. Nobody would have given it a second thought. But instead he said she looked terrific, and maybe ogled her a little, as a fellow is apt to do in a weak or careless moment. And for the next couple of years his only conversations are with lawyers.

In the newsroom of a past era, we harassed each other all the time. It wasn't overtly sexual, but you can bet that was in the back of our minds. Boy reporters deviled and insulted girl reporters by asking them to go up to the corner saloon after the final edition went to print, or sometimes before it did. Girl reporters harassed and tormented boy reporters by telling them to get lost.

It was not then regarded as necessary to be neutered before entering the journalism trade, so this shameful byplay went on pretty much all the time. If we'd been prosecuted for it, we'd have spent most of our careers at the courthouse and there'd have been nobody left to get the paper out.

From direct experience, I'm of the belief that there's nowhere near as much sexual harassment going on today as some people would have you believe.

I spend a lot of time standing around in locations where I think there might be some action. I position myself next to the water fountain, or by the coffee machine on the next floor up, and try to look receptive. When a young woman heads toward me, I am thinking *Hot diggety! Here comes my ticket to a fancy settlement.* But all they ever say is, "Excuse me," or "Move it, Pops." And nowhere in those remarks, try as I might, can I find a double-entendre.

It is consoling to imagine that some of these woman co-workers must from time to time be sorely tempted to sexually harass me. But in today's litigious climate, what no doubt holds them back is their fear that I might interpret a sultry leer — or even common civility — as an affront worth prosecuting.

Well, I am of the old school, brought up in the bawdier newsroom of yesteryear, and I want to go on record here as telling them they have nothing in the world to worry about. After all I've been through, not even to mention my age, sexual harassment would have to be of a most aggravated kind before I noticed anything was happening.

And by then I hope I'd be gentleman enough not to complain.

ANYONE YOU KNOW?

The newspaper and TV screens in our town have been decorated, of late, with an artist's drawing of the face of a man being hunted in a series of despicable crimes against children.

Such portraiture, composed from the descriptions of witnesses and victims — in this case, child victims — is at very best an approximation. There is a fair probability it somewhat resembles the criminal. Given the infinite variety of faces, it is all but certain to look exactly like someone else.

Shortly after the first publication of the picture, I was visiting with a group of people at an event in another town. They all were journalists and college teachers — people of some standing, not roving pedophiles. Midway in this affair, I spied in the back of the room a face that looked familiar. *Where do I know that fellow from?* I thought.

Then it came to me: *Why, he looks a whole lot like that guy they're hunting for.*

It was a fair distance from the platform to the rear row where he sat. And my far eyesight isn't what it once was.

But there was no mistaking the similarity. So I was presented with a nice little moral and legal problem: Should I stop in mid-phrase and shout out, "Seize that man! Yes, *that* one! The perverted devil with the mustache and box haircut"? Or would it be better to wait until the program ended, then send for authorities so the rascal could be collared at his lunch?

In fact, I did nothing.

I am not indifferent about the molestation of little girls. My own daughters were small once, and if anyone had attacked them I would have done my level best to inflict a severity of punishment the law does not allow. But I was remembering, in that moment, an afternoon years ago, when I was traveling on assignment for the newspaper.

I went into the post office of a small Georgia town to mail a letter, and my eye happened to wander to the bulletin board beside the clerk's window. Among the "Wanted" bulletins, I saw a photograph of myself — or someone who could have been my identical twin. He was being sought on warrants for mail robbery and aggravated assault, the poster said, and should be considered armed and extremely dangerous. I finished my business at the postal window. Then, hunkering as far down as possible in the car seat, I hied myself out of that wretched place.

And that was a photograph. A composite drawing presents the opportunity for even greater error. No power on earth could have persuaded me to finger the unlucky professor or editor sitting in the back of the lecture hall.

That old memory came back again when I read, just a few days ago, about how a furious mob set upon and severely beat a young man whose only offense was to bear a slight facial resemblance to the drawing being circulated by police. He was, of course, a perfect innocent. And there's the nightmare. Any one of us, any day, could wake up resembling the published picture of some demon on the prowl.

"Bearded," says the victim, and the artist draws in a beard. *"Short . . . pudgy . . . balding . . . shifty-eyed. Dressed like a rag-picker."* The pen and brush do their work faithfully.

And I'd recognize the monster anywhere. I see him every morning in the mirror.

TYRONE'S LUCKY DAY

It was just a little item in the news, but an engaging one — about how they made a mistake with prisoner Tyrone Simmons out there in Washington state. "It's time to go," they told Simmons when they came early to wake him in his cell. "Who, me?" he said. "Are you sure?"

They were sure.

It's time to go. Isn't that what the warden always says when they're ready to lead some rascal off to the execution chamber? But there was no shout of "Dead man walking!" No priest in attendance and no spectators watching from behind glass.

Instead, they handed him $30 in cash and some personal items, and opened the door to the street. Tyrone Simmons, who'd been held for investigation of theft and drug possession, was a free man. Just one problem. He was the *wrong* Simmons. The man they were supposed to release was another prisoner with the same last name.

So now the hunt's on for poor Tyrone. When and if he's caught, they say he'll be charged for his "escape." The fault was his, the jail director contends. It wasn't enough just to ask them if they had the right man. Tyrone ought to have objected more strenuously to being let go. Isn't that the establishment for you? Always looking for a fall guy for its own mistakes.

I was reminded, as I read the item, of a story some time back about a bank's unfortunate blunder.

Somehow, a computer operator working after hours to enter the day's transactions in the system hit a wrong key. When the bank opened for business the next morning, several of its customers found they had a few extra millions in their accounts.

Now I'm as honest as the next man. If a sales clerk hands me my change, with a $5 bill accidentally mixed in among the ones, I invariably say, "You might want to count that again." If, after ordering dessert at a restaurant, I notice the waiter has neglected to add the Double-Chocolate Obscenity to my bill, I call the oversight immediately to his or her attention.

These small acts of integrity leave one feeling wonderfully righteous. What's more, they are apt to be remembered and may earn you special consideration the next time you visit that establishment.

So far, however, I have not been severely tested.

I have banked with the same institution for 40-some years. They are fine people, many of them friends, and the relationship has been mutually beneficial. They have covered my overdrafts, and I have paid them a great deal of interest. But I am herewith putting them on notice. I cannot say with absolute certainty *what* I would do if one month I were to receive my statement and find, through some computer hiccup, they had added six extra zeros to my balance.

In this age of electronic finance, an instantaneous transfer to a numbered account in the Cayman Islands is easily accomplished. There are any number of countries in the world where one might arrange quite a pleasant life, without being inconvenienced by reciprocal extradition treaties.

Like Tyrone Simmons, I would, of course, *try* to do the honorable thing. I would present myself at the teller's window. "If you wouldn't mind," I'd say, "could you please verify my account number?"

And then, like Tyrone, I just might *walk*.

ME AND IBRAHIM

I read that American farming has become a modern industry, just like any other. But I know nothing about that. My practice of it has more in common with the struggles of the Third World. When I go to the field, I could be making a documentary for U.S. aid on subsistence agriculture in the upper Niger basin.

First the ancient tractor must be persuaded to run.

Narration: Ibrahim Odingwe is the first man in his vil-

lage of nine families to possess such a machine. It is an old tractor, but he is very proud of it. He does not understand the principle of the internal combustion engine. He believes that only rituals and incantations will make his tractor run.

Once started, it operates only intermittently. When the motor dies, elaborate measures are required to get the thing running again.

Narration: The saving of labor is enormous. Ibrahim used to farm in the way of his father and his father's father. Using his wives to pull the implements, it took five days to cultivate his small field. With the tractor, it takes only three days. This frees Ibrahim's wives for such recreation as child-bearing and the processing of wild roots.

My friend Patrick participated in my most recent farming venture. The day was cloudy and cool, fine for working. With the worn-out disc, it required at least a dozen passes over the ground to prepare a primitive seedbed. "What next?" Patrick said.

"We fertilize."

"Yes, but how?"

"Why, by hand, of course."

Narration: Before the river went dry, Ibrahim fertilized his little plot with fish. Now there are no fish. He must use precious chemical fertilizer, which he applies with care, employing the technology of an empty soup can. As he flings out his arm with each step, he recites a prayer to the gods of his ancestors.

"While I'm finishing this," I said, "why don't you bring the seed? It's in a sack in a barrel in the shed."

After a while Patrick came back with the seed. "It's spoiled."

"What do you mean, *spoiled?*"

"See, it's full of bugs. They've eaten half or more of it."

Narration: For Ibrahim and his people, survival is at the mercy of rodents and weevils.

"Never mind," I said. "We'll just plant more of it."

"How do we do it?"

"Like the fertilizer, by hand. We'll mix the seed with dirt. That way it will go farther."

"I hate to think how long that's going to take," Patrick said.

Narration: For farmers like Ibrahim, time is without meaning.

The day drew far on. The ground was cultivated, fertilized and seeded. Both of us were stooped with exhaustion. "Now we have to get the seed covered. I'll go cut a tree," I said.

"You'll what?"

"Cut a tree to drag behind the tractor. It's a keen way to work the seed in."

Narration: Habit is powerful, and change comes slowly. Progress in the upper Niger basin is at war with centuries-old ways.

Evening was coming on. Our pitiful labors were concluded. The field was planted, and it even was possible something might grow there. And the only difference between my farm and Ibrahim's is that, in the middle United States, there's a slightly better chance of rain.

HIS PRAIRIE HANDS

I met a man once who had devoted much of a prairie life to taking stones out of fields and laying up stone walls around his land. Many years afterward, when great age had enfeebled him, it was that work of which he was proud above all other. To look at his walls still gave him pleasure.

He spread his hands palms-up as he sat buried under robes in the chair from which he scarcely could stand to walk. The rest of him was frail. But the hands, though gnarled, had a surprising look of strength. Even to that day, he said, they could remember the feel of the stones.

I was very young, then, and understood practically nothing about anything. So I took the old man's tale of fields and walls for so much wistful exaggeration.

Subsequently I have had occasion to try the thing he spoke of — the first part of it, at least; the picking up, if not the building — and have, as a result, a clearer idea of the dimensions of that man's life.

The field I lately had to clear was not properly a field at all, more a small meadow, steeply sloping so that the ground could not be plowed without the risk of causing ditches. Worthless as it lay, its sod exhausted, we had thought to plant new grass directly into the unbroken soil. However, the equipment for that is of an expensive kind, not commonly owned. Another man was bringing his to do the planting for us. And it seemed advisable to spend a part of a day gathering up stones to lessen the risk of damage to his machine.

A friend helped begin the job. The meadow, as I say, was small — four acres at the most. By the end of the first day we had gotten over half of it or a bit less.

The smaller stones we threw together in piles for later loading. The larger ones we rolled to the piles or manhandled together to the meadow's edge. The stones themselves came to have a personality. Some sly ones showed just a tip above the ground. But when the time came for dislodging them — we used a heavy steel bar for a pry — they might be large as half a bushel.

It is parching, back-wrenching labor, even in the mildness of a spring morning. By afternoon it is nearly unbearable. One clears a small area, four or five steps square, and throws the gatherings in a heap, then straightens with a groan to survey the next such square and find it, if possible, stonier than the last.

What seemed at the start so slight a scrap of land comes to be a major part of the planet's surface. By sundown the two of us were staggering like drunks, our hands blistered from all the grubbing and lifting.

The second day I worked mostly alone, with only someone to drive the tractor that pulled a wagon behind. The piles we'd made the previous day I threw onto the wagon. And later, at the meadow's lower end, threw off again. The piles, with some new stones I picked up or pried out, amounted in all to three wagon loads.

At that, the work in the four acres was not finished. But just as evening was deepening toward night, and when a sly rock of unexpected heft had brought me whimpering to my knees, it occurred to me in a flash of sudden revelation that the meadow, while not quite clear of stones, was as clear as it was ever going to be in my ownership.

So we took the wagon down and emptied it, and I looked at the proof of my accomplishment. Two days' work, three wagon loads. Taken all together, my pile would not have sufficed to build 10 steps of a decent wall.

Standing there in a stupor of exhaustion, I thought of a wall running perhaps a half-mile along a wooded ridge nearby — an antique construction of forgotten purpose. Thought of other stone fences, more distant ones and longer, flung out along Scottish country lanes to the very end of seeing.

And thought finally of that prairie man I'd met, broken in his chair, and of how one might afterward feel to have cleared and then walled a pasture measured not in paces but in miles and parts of miles.

His hands, he said, in the understated way of heroes, remembered the stones. Just that. And shortly afterward he died.

THE MEDICINE MAN

Our expatriate daughter called in a panic from New York. Something was wrong with her foot. "I got up in the morning, and it hurt so much I almost couldn't stand on it."

"Have you seen a doctor?"

"Yes. He says he can fix it. He wants to break the bones in both my feet."

"He *what?* Who is this guy? Does he wear jackboots and

speak with a Teutonic accent?"

"Somebody gave me his name," she said.

"Listen very carefully," I told her. "Stay calm, but get out of there any way you can. Tell him you need to use the restroom. When you get down to the street, take a cab or flag a police car — anything. You may be in great danger."

"It's all right," she said. "I'm at home."

"That's a relief. Don't go near that creep again."

"I won't. I have the name of another doctor. I'm seeing him on Wednesday."

When we heard from her after that second appointment, her voice was bright. "He's good," she said. "Some of his patients are dancers. He knows a lot about feet."

"So what was it?"

"A problem in the joint of my little toe," she said.

"And?"

"He gave me a shot of cortisone. When I walked out it was fine."

"That's all?"

"It's over. It doesn't hurt a bit. He said he would give me some exercises to strengthen the joint."

It's an alarming little story. Two unknown doctors in a distant city containing millions of people, some of them reasonably weird. One wants to cure the patient by breaking bones, with weeks on crutches and follow-up visits that could last a year. The other corrects the problem in 15 minutes with a shot.

Clearly medicine is as much art as science. And it's fair to say there's risk in every field. Fall in with the wrong kind of journalist, for example, and he'll do worse than break your feet. He'll break your reputation and trash your life.

So whom do you trust? That's the question always, but especially when you're in some place far from your support system of known people.

Ten years ago in Africa I got a worm in my foot. The Lebanese doctor I saw put some tablets in a small, unmarked envelope. "Take these," he said. "You'll feel terrible, but they won't kill you. They'll only kill the worm."

I looked in his eyes, and saw there the assurance of a man who knew his business.

The worm perished. I did not.

Another time, years before that, the salad *nicoise* in a Moscow hotel restaurant smote me with stomach cramps of such violence as to make death seem almost attractive. A Russian doctor treated me, without effect, and in that condition I had to fly off to Samarkand.

"Take this," said an Uzbek taxi driver, and gave me a dusty brown lozenge larger than a nickel. He seemed a man of good will. I chewed and swallowed the thing, and the next day was fully restored.

When you're out there on your own — in some Third World backwater or, as in my daughter's case, in the wilderness of New York — you have to depend on hunches and intuition to get you through. But if you have a hurting toe, and the good doctor proposes to fix it by breaking both your feet, there's reason to suspect it's time for a second opinion.

VIII

A TERROR TAMED

Eric, the tuxedo cat, loves his 15 minutes each morning under the front-yard bushes, consorting amiably with the rabbit that comes to visit.

But somewhere out there *the Orange Peril waits!* The provenance of that swaggering beast is unknown. He must be a member of some other household in the neighborhood, for his passage across our lawn is a fairly regular event. At home he may be coddled and adored. Here he is despised.

Eric will be perched on the inner window sill, sniffing the spring air, watching birds. Then, out of nowhere — like an apparition from an evil dream — the enormous orange tabby will come lumbering by. He looks up at the window. Their stares meet. Eric trembles with fury at the trespass. Once the intruder sprang up to hang by his claws from the window screen. But usually, after determining he's been satisfactorily noticed, the orange one just gives a kind of shrug and passes on.

One morning last week, Eric had gone out with me as he usually does when I fetch the paper. A short time later, as I sat reading over the day's first cup of coffee, there arose from outside the front door a violent commotion — spitting, screeching, yowling, and other noises I hadn't known a cat could make. Rushing there, I flung open the door and Eric came scuttling in, low to the ground.

At the eye's corner, I caught just a glimpse of the orange brute making his hasty way toward other parts. So they'd met whisker to whisker at last. No injuries were detected. The battle seemed to have been mainly one of shouted insults. But it has changed the nature of our mornings.

Each day, since then, Eric has gone to the door as usual, asking for his quarter-hour at large. The door is opened. From the safety of the hall, he peers out with a mix of longing and apprehension. Then, sadly, he turns away.

I understand, and know what he's feeling. Because there was a threat like that in my own early boyhood as well. In the first grade, I think it was, or possibly the second, there was a boy the same age, but a good deal larger, who found pleasure in deviling me on the way home from school. He'd twist my arm behind my back, and march me around, his helpless prisoner, sometimes all the way to his house before releasing me to flee to mine. Each morning I left for school in an agony of dread, knowing the torment that might wait at the end of the day.

It happened only a few times, and eventually it stopped. He found another victim, or turned to pulling the legs off bugs. I met that fellow years later, and am glad to say he'd outgrown such meanness. That could happen to the prowling tabby, too, maybe sooner rather than later.

So today, when Eric turned away from the door again in despair, I snatched him up and carried him out onto the stoop. He surveyed the yard. The orange thug was nowhere to be seen. So he went on out, then, to wait under his bush for the companionship of the resident rabbit. He stayed his full 15 minutes, and had to be called three times. When finally he came, his manner seemed more confident. There was a bounce in his step. And I suspect he's already looking forward to tomorrow's outing.

For all of us, life contains a variety of terrors — some that are unbearable in the imagining. But they tend to get smaller the sooner you're able to face them.

PITY THE WORKING MAN

As the baseball season slides into another August of mediocrity, I have given up reading the sports pages. One gets a craw full, finally, of the whining and excuse-making.

Men who receive millions of dollars in salary to hit thrown balls or catch batted ones turn out to be much better at talking. They wax eloquent as they explain the difficulty of doing what they are paid to do. You would almost think, sometimes, that the game of baseball was something they stumbled into by accident.

The ball just isn't jumping off their bats like it should. The opposing pitcher had a performance of freakish brilliance. The ball a fielder dropped didn't fly true the way it should — it was fluttering and knuckling. The wind blew from an unfavorable quarter. The fans were ignorant and unsupportive.

Some ballplayers have more explanations than failed politicians. Others don't talk at all. Hungry for attention when times are good, they become mute and surly in defeat. Occasionally, in their frustration, men getting on toward middle age — with superb physiques and minds uncluttered by reflection — fall upon one another like playground hotheads.

Especially do I tire of their attempts at self-analysis. For some reason, they just aren't "feeling good" at the plate or in the field. Their confidence has mysteriously evaporated. So has their enthusiasm. In spite of being compensated, as a team, by an amount greater than the gross national product of certain republics, they can't seem to get "interested."

The reasons for this malaise are elusive. But it is profound. And the impression, from all the ink it receives, is that the fate of the West hangs in the balance, awaiting their emotional recovery.

Bullfrogs! I cried aloud the other morning, flinging the sports page aside for what I vow will be the last time this season. I've had enough of dilettante millionaires in knickers. And strangely, then, Ernie popped into my mind.

Ernie is our friend, who carries the mail daily on our route. And I feel good every time I see him coming. Whether it's through blistering heat or sleet and a cutting wind, he swings along our block with the brisk, confident stride of a man who's needed, is pleased with what he does, who sets high standards for himself and makes a habit of meeting them.

His is at least as physical a job as any ballplayer's. Ballplayers spend half their time sitting down, and most of the other half bent over with hands on knees, working their jaws and spitting. Ernie will last a career through, I'd bet on it. Because he's fit, and works at staying that way.

Oh, I'm sure he has his bad days. Frustrations and disappointments and sudden griefs — they come to anyone. But Ernie's aren't reported in the newspaper, and solemnly dissected. Nor would you know it from seeing him on his route. He has a job to do. And in his consistently friendly and optimistic way, he goes about doing it. Because, unlike ballplayers, people *depend* on him.

A letter bearing someone's thoughts and feelings, bills from creditors, contracts to be executed, news of some small success — all these and a thousand others pass through his hands, and those of his postal colleagues, every day. And they are important. Lives could be wrecked if they went astray.

Ballplayers, on the other hand, could fall into a fit of thumb-sucking, choke on their cuds of tobacco, fail to show up for work — every last one of them. Franchises could collapse, uniforms mildew and rot and the hot summer winds blow through the dark tunnels of empty stadiums. And, except in some abstract, nostalgic way, no one really would care. Life would not change at all.

Being able to last the course at what you do has some connection, I'm bound to think, with doing work that really counts.

THE WEIGHT OF MEMORY

Five crows appeared on the lawn this morning just at the first daylight hour. Swaggering, broad-shouldered fellows they were — glossy, vain, independent.

I went out to fetch the paper from the walk. With an indignant croak, the crows levitated onto a branch of the neighbor's maple tree, waited until the nuisance of me had disappeared, then flapped down to continue their prospecting. They must be part of the larger flock — the immense crow congregation — that roosts somewhere nearby, but usually is seen at dawn and dusk, rowing across the still pond of the sky, bound to or from outlying fields.

Grain has begun to ripen. With grasshoppers hopping and cicadas humming and farmers greasing their machines in readiness for the harvest that's almost at hand, this is the season of plenty in the country. Why those five would stop off to spend most of an hour in a city yard I can't guess.

But there they strutted, and sometimes spoke. And the coarseness of their voices alarmed the tuxedo cat who, when I came back with the paper, was waiting nervously, to be let inside.

From the safety of the window ledge he watched them. And from my window, I've watched them as I worked. Common they may be. But they are intelligent, as birds go. Handsome and able in flight, even on the ground they have a kind of sleek elegance about them. I can never see crows near at hand without feeling a little twinge of sorrow

— regret about something remembered, something that happened more than 40 years ago.

Only once in a lifetime of hunting have I ever aimed a gun at something I did not intend to eat.

It happened one frigid twilight during a winter I was spending alone in a woodland cabin. I'd tromped a cold hour or two looking for a squirrel for supper, but squirrels were scarce that year and I was coming back with nothing for the pan. A solitary crow, no doubt a laggard from his group, came over the trees ahead of me, black against the last lemon light.

For no reason I could afterward explain, even to myself — simply with that carelessness of someone who hadn't yet had enough losses to know the value of anything — I swung the gun and fired.

It was a random, utterly purposeless thing. And I was startled when the bird spun awkwardly down almost at my feet. I remember the guilt I felt in that moment, and in the days afterward as I tried, without success, to splint and heal the broken wing and thereby earn some kind of absolution. The crow would have none of my clumsy penitence. He fixed me furiously with his amber eye. And each night, while I slept, he tore the bandage off again.

It ended badly, as such things generally do. Some wrongs are without remedy, some cruelties past mending. I buried the poor feathered thing at the edge of the cabin clearing. Even now, half a life later, I know the exact place. And while there's no redeeming so sad and pointless an affair, I believe I learned from it a young man's first lesson in the certainty of consequences.

The crows that came to my lawn this morning do not

know, of course, what happened at that woods edge on an evening 40-some years ago. But I know. The past never can be entirely put behind. What we have done is part of what we are, and will be with us always — as this memory has stayed with me.

How much accumulated weight of deliberate or careless wrong is one prepared to carry? In the end, that calculation governs the decisions of a life.

SALVATION'S SIDE DOOR

A mong my few virtues, promptness ranks foremost. It is the result, almost surely, of years spent in an occupation governed by the clock. Journalists are obsessively devoted to deadlines, and in all that time I have never missed one. Although the fear of it is very great.

I cannot say what would happen to me — to my self-regard and my competence — if ever this rule were to be breached. But I suspect that punctuality in a journalist is a requirement of character as absolute as honesty in a bank clerk or chastity in a nun. And that if I were ever to deliver a story late — even once — that first small lapse would be followed by an appallingly rapid slide into dissolution and harlotry.

Now there are, I must admit, certain persons — more than a few of them — to whom this news of my promptness may come as a considerable surprise. The minister of the church, for one.

The first service of the morning begins at 9 o'clock. I

imagine that other families make a point of arriving several minutes early and chatting companionably in the outer corridors before making their leisurely way to the pews. I only *imagine* this. I have never been there nearly in time actually to observe it.

Providentially, there is a side door through which the tardy and other backsliders may arrive, their entrance observed by not more than one-third of the assembled congregation. It is the only door I know. Yesterday our family slunk in at half past the hour, during the singing of the last hymn before the minister rose to speak.

A neighbor attends the same service, and from Sunday to Sunday it is touch and go which of us will be the last to be seated. Yesterday was no contest. Our neighbor was in his place and had gotten his wind back and was looking straight ahead, like someone who might have been there overnight.

Other communicants, being people of charitable heart, pretend not to notice. But I must believe that in some way these scandalous arrivals are being remembered and marked down against us.

What needs to be known is that in this, as in most else, I am blameless. I get out of bed when called, and select a suit of clothes — the winter one or the summer one, depending on the season — and am standing beside the door, car keys in hand, at the proper hour. But example is useless. My wife is incapable of fast movement at that hour. When badgered about time, she becomes flustered and resentful.

I remember how, in my daughters' girlhood years, clothes and grooming were of huge moment. From the upper reaches of the house could be heard the splashing of water and the slow purring of hair dryers and exclamations of dismay as various parts of intended costumes were found either to be in disharmony or in the laundry.

Time passed. You would not believe how *much* time passed. The breakfast I had lovingly prepared would grow cold. Milk curdled in the glasses. The eggs congealed.

I would get a book. Nearly all my reading has been done while waiting to go to church. Over the years, if I had used that time to read theological tracts and explications, it would not have been necessary for me to go to church at all. I would already have been a very learned and possibly a very holy man.

We're doing the best we can! would come the distant cries. And, sadly, it was true. *Get out our coats!*

That command about the coats always made my heart leap up. It suggested we would be leaving that same day. Then the neighbor's car would start, and he would drive hastily up the street and out of hearing in the direction of the church. And I would know there was no hope of respectability left.

Someday, I assumed, my daughters would discover the function of clocks and the importance of timeliness in the pursuit of an orderly life. Before then, however, their career interest likely would have taken shape. And I prayed it would not be an interest in the journalist's trade.

I prayed that most earnestly on Sunday mornings. Salvation being the work of a lifetime, the minister is necessarily a patient man. But I have known ministers and I have known managing editors. And the resemblance between them is not usually large.

A COUNTRY FRIEND

The country dog is a merry pup.

Sergeant, I would call him, if he were mine to name, because everything that happens along that stretch of country road comes under his supervision. His sharp eyes — one bluish-white, one brown — miss nothing. He knows the cars and trucks that regularly pass. He travels on tireless young legs and naps where it pleases him. His days contain the possibility of many meals.

He has a regular home, a base of operations, but his idea of family is inclusive. He has taken me for one of his people, and regards my cabin and my woods as extensions of his place across the road. If I turn in the drive after an absence of days or weeks, he is there immediately. If I sit on the cabin porch to write at some peculiar hour of early morning, just as the light has begun to come, I look up from the work to find him bedded outside, peering in.

His hearing must be fabulous. The sound of my door opening — no matter how quietly I try to do it — brings him flying straight as a wire. And at supper time, if I'm turning a piece of meat over the fire on the open grate, I can count on his undivided attention. He knows that when the man eats steak, happy moments are apt to follow for a country pup.

The city dog, my old friend, Rufus, used to go with me often to the farm. He had achieved the mellowness of years. Legs that used to carry him swift as a bird to the farthest wood line were slowed by hurts and age. But he loved the outdoors still. And I took him for the company — him riding beside me on the front seat, as long service entitled him to do.

I wondered if there might be a problem with the country pup, that new dog from across the road, whom he hadn't met before. But I worried needlessly. Though there are brutes and outlaws among them, as in any species, the society of dogs on the whole is at least as civil as ours.

Rufus bounded from the car. The pup was waiting. They introduced themselves, in the earthy way dogs do. Rufus circled the cabin clearing, placing his proprietary mark on several trees. And with these ceremonies concluded, they set off together into the woods.

I could catch glimpses of them through the trees and undergrowth — one white with black spots, the other a happy splash of white and orange. They checked back from time to time, breathless and grinning, to be sure I hadn't gotten lost. Then, when Rufus had had enough of running, he led the country dog down the path to the pond.

Through the reeds he plunged and the spotted pup, after just a moment's hesitation, followed. They swam a half-circle out into deep water and back again. Then came to me where I was sitting on the dock and, one on either side, shook themselves until I was satisfactorily wet.

After that we went up to the cabin. They were nosing at the wood pile. And I, occupied with some little task inside, was inattentive for a moment. When I looked again, the two of them were gone. I walked to the end of my lane and saw them then, bounding side by side through a meadow on the road's far side. Rufus, after sharing his woods and pond, had been invited across to explore the territory of the pup.

Worn out by all these fine excursions, the city dog slept on the rug while the typewriter clicked. The country dog sat at the screen door, waiting for the next romp — or maybe waiting for me to start a fire in the grill.

Their people friends are good and useful, but creatures appreciate the company of their own kind. And though it wasn't my plan, it looked very much as if we'd become a family.

WHAT IS SCIENCE, REALLY?

Just before daylight the other morning I saw a bunch of men jostling and shouldering for a place in line outside a drugstore. Curious, I stopped and asked one of them what the commotion was all about.

He showed me a piece torn out of the morning paper about a new potion, just approved by the Food and Drug Administration, for growing hair on balding heads. It was still four hours before the store opened. And the drug wouldn't be available in pharmacies for at least another month, the article said. But the men in the line weren't taking any chances.

I wished the fellow luck and got out of there in a hurry. Once the sun came up, the glare from all those scalps could do serious damage to the unprotected eye.

This may be the medical breakthrough of the century but, frankly, I'm not much interested. I still had, at last count, 12 hairs directly on top. Carefully arranged and fixed in place with bear grease, they get me through the day without humiliation. Years ago, a highly educated friend with a graduate degree from Oxford told me that balding in men was the sign of a powerful libido. He was getting hairless then, and I wasn't. But I promised myself that if I ever noticed my own hair falling out I would just accept it as pure undeserved good luck.

Anyway, an ointment able to restore hair must be very strong indeed. There may be risks still not known. For instance, what if you spilled some of it and had to spend the next five years shaving your shoes?

These are minor cavils, you say. And probably you are right. Because it is clear that the global demand for this preparation is going to be huge. From the marketing standpoint, it is almost a perfect product. It could take four to six months of application before the user knows if it's doing him any good. And, if it works, he must continue the treatment for a lifetime or else the regenerated hair will fall out.

We are talking here about a license to print money!

That's how it is with research, though. Some people get the glory and the big dollars, and some people work a lifetime without ever having their work recognized or their names in the medical journals.

As a small boy, I was bothered badly with poison ivy. If I even looked at the weed, I erupted in blisters all over and itched so bad I couldn't sit in school or even sleep. My parents would take me, then, to a medicine man they knew — the aged father of a friend of theirs. He lived in a shack in the swampy, wooded valley of a creek just past where the city ended and the country began.

I remember him as a wonderful and reclusive character, with a shapeless felt hat and rough clothes and an aura of pipe smoke about him. In his shack he made herbal concoctions for a variety of ailments. The one for poison ivy he got from crushed green walnut husks. There may have been other ingredients, but that was the main one.

He put up the medicine in little jars with hand-lettered labels, and it stank like anything. But one thing sure: It *worked*. Rub on that brown juice, and in a day or two — no matter how bad the case — the itching stopped completely and the blisters dried and began to heal.

That was most of 50 years ago. The city has grown far beyond there, now. The road beside the creek leads to a shopping mall. There are baseball fields on one side, and a factory on the other, and the housing subdivisions spread across the hills beyond. Whenever I happen to drive that way I always think of the little man who lived in the shack in the woods, squeezing walnuts and saving me a world of misery.

He lived an uncelebrated life and died unknown, and wasted his time fixing hurts when he might have made it big doing something really important, like growing fuzz on balding heads. In science, as in most else, fame is luck and timing.

As the Season Turns

Both daughters were home this year for the Orange Barrel Festival, and I was pleased they could make it.

"I think you caught the color at its peak," I told them. Some people travel hundreds of miles for the Fall Leaf Festival in Vermont, or the Covered Bridge Festival in Indiana, or the Azalea Festival in Wilmington, N.C.

People in our town are lucky. We don't have to go anywhere, because the spectacle is right here at home.

"Now you see what you've been missing," I said.

They agreed it was pretty amazing.

"The whole city is a riot of orange," one of them said. "I didn't know there were this many orange barrels in the whole world."

"That's what makes it special. Lots of towns have a few of them, but that's hardly worth seeing. You need to get them massed by the thousands to create the real effect."

"Is there a tour?"

"Many," I said. "They're self-guided. All you have to do is start south on Main Street. When you come to the first *Detour* sign, that's where one tour begins. Or you can try to get on the interstate at 103rd Street. That's another tour.

"Actually," I told them, "it doesn't much matter which direction you go. You're sure to find one. You'll see cars backed up for several blocks, all going about three miles an hour. Four lanes of traffic will squeeze down to one. The color orange will predominate. And you'll know you've joined a tour."

"It must take a lot of planning."

"Yes, that's the impressive part. If you just had orange barrels on one street, people would get used to them and take another route, and all you'd have is a minor nuisance. The trick is to *anticipate*. If you have barrels on all the streets at once, then you have a festival."

"How long does the festival go on?" they wanted to know.

"It's pretty much a continuous affair," I said. "Unless the money runs out."

"You mean there'll be orange barrels on all the streets forever?"

"For the rest of our natural lives."

"It must cost a lot."

"Not so much, when you think of the tourism dollars it attracts. People come through on their way to New Orleans or California and wind up spending a week or two here because they get caught in a tour and can't find their way out of town. They sleep in hotels. They eat in restaurants. It pumps millions into the local economy. Also, there's the gambling."

"The what?"

"You know, the floating casinos down on the river. Eventually gambling will finance everything — schools, the Orange Barrel Festival, domed stadiums, politicians' junkets, universal health care, lethal injections. There won't even have to be taxes."

"Well," they said, "we won't be here to see it."

"What do you mean?"

"We'll probably be living somewhere else."

"Nonsense," I told them. "All the highways are blocked. There's no way out. That's the whole point of the Orange Barrel Festival."

GATHERING HER FLOCK

In the cool of early morning, as the coffee is heating, I hear her at the far back of the yard, calling out through the gate.

Her voice is sweet — inviting, entreating. She is calling the name of the smallest cat, the gray one, who, although grown matronly and dignified, still has a yen for explorations.

In the early years, it satisfied the little cat to investigate the bushes of the yard. Then she took to ascending the redbud tree to the garage roof, crouching there henlike and mewing pitifully for rescue. We kept a ladder handy, and climbing up to fetch her was my regular chore before going to the office.

Then we put in what's called a privacy fence — not to keep the world out but to keep our legions in. Between the old fence, which was on the rear property line, and the new wooden one, which is set in a couple of feet, is a narrow no-man's land I've never dared to enter. The fence installers sprayed that strip with chemicals that were supposed to keep the vegetation down. But the weeds on my land are unwholesomely vigorous. They thrive on poison.

I opened the gate and looked in there once. It's impenetrable — a jungle of such density that, if the pioneers had seen anything like it when they looked west, the settlement of America would have ended at New Jersey.

But that's now the small gray cat's terrain of choice. She has found a space under the gate just large enough to squeeze through. And for a quarter-hour each early morning she disappears into the trackless hinterland. I suppose I could fill the place with earth, or perhaps put a stone there to block the way. But she'd just go back to climbing on the garage roof. As it is, she doesn't venture far, and it seems a pity to prevent so inexpensive and innocent a pleasure.

What's more, the morning routine has become part of the pattern of our lives. I enjoy hearing my wife call her.

"Gray," she croons. *"Come, Gray."* She speaks the name with a kind of musical trill. Sometimes I hear her say, mock-scoldingly, *"There you are! All right, come now."* But that's a bluff, I can tell. She's pretending the little cat's already seen, when that isn't so at all.

Eventually, though, the wanderer does appear from out of the vines and saplings, and is gathered up in arms. I can hear the rattle of the gate being closed and latched. Then, just as the coffee is made and the first cup poured, I can see them through the kitchen window coming back across the yard — a girl carrying the first cat of her childhood and all the cats since, a shepherd bringing the errant one safely back to fold.

It is one small, dependable note of victory upon which to begin each day.

What luck to be a creature who's accounted for and prized, and whose adventures will never take you beyond the reach of that sweet voice. How reassuring too, for me, to share house and yard and cat and life with one so faithful in the seeking.

THE FAINTING COUCH

A daughter is relocating to more spacious lodgings and is desperate for furniture to fill the place. It means for us, the parents, an opportunity to unload some things we no longer need. There's even a chance that, in time, I might once again have use of the garage.

Among the pieces we let go was a low, daybed kind of affair that I've always heard spoken of as the *fainting couch*. In my memory, no one around here has ever fainted. But nevertheless that's what it's been called: the fainting couch.

My wife brought this curiosity to our marriage, along with her white cat, and it served as our first sofa. There's no knowing how many friends it may have cost us. For while it would be ideal for use by anyone who has just lost consciousness, it's an agony to sit upon.

Either you perch on the front edge, without any support for your back. Or it can be placed against a wall. But then, if people of normal height are to take advantage of the wall's support, they must sit with their legs thrust out straight before them, like infants in a highchair or dolls on a shelf.

In later years — the last 25 or so — it has been in an upstairs back room that briefly was my writing place, but then evolved into a catch-all storage area. No sooner had the thing been carted away than my wife announced plans for the space thus liberated.

"I'd like to bring the sewing machine up from the basement," she said.

If we hadn't already given away the fainting couch, I might have used it right then!

"What in heaven's name for?" I screeched. The sewing machine is of the treadle kind, manufactured by the Singer company and very popular 50 or 100 years ago, but found now only in the thatched huts and sweatshops of Third World countries.

Or in basements like ours.

"Why would you want that upstairs?" I demanded to know.

"Because," she said defiantly. "I might want to sew."

"But you *hate* sewing!"

In a girlhood project — for home economics class, it must have been — she set out to make some simple garment, but ripped out seams and restitched them so many times that, before she could finish it, the fabric just *disintegrated*.

She has many gifts, but sewing is not among them.

"You're about as likely to use that machine as I am to take up plumbing," I said.

She considered that.

"No," she said. "I'm *more* likely."

She was, of course, alluding to the drippy bathroom faucet, about which I once recklessly observed that all it needed was a new washer. From that moment, hardly a day has passed when she has not asked if I intend to replace the faucet washer.

"I don't think we have any washers on hand," I tell her.

"Then you'll have to get one, won't you? Probably at the hardware store."

"First I'll have to find out the size."

"You could measure the old one."

"Yes, and I'll do it, too," I tell her. "One of these days."

The truth is, I haven't any clear notion at all about how one goes about changing a faucet washer. Or if the washers come in different sizes. Or if that model faucet even *has* one. I'm bluffing — just as she's bluffing about taking up sewing.

You sometimes hear that marriage is two people combining their strengths. But we've come together, merging our baggage of weaknesses, and somehow we've made a life.

GET THE COLOR RIGHT

"You're picking at your salad again," said my wife. It is an offense that rarely escapes notice.

"I'm not either *picking*. I'm simply being selective."

"But you've selected out all the carrots."

"Yes, well, I prefer not to eat unnatural foods."

"Carrots are perfectly natural," she said.

"That's where you're wrong. The natural color of carrots is purple. These are mutants."

"Where did you get a crazy idea like that?"

"I read it in the paper a couple of weeks ago. It said carrots were purple for hundreds of years, until somebody decided to breed them for orange."

"I'd like to see that article," she said.

"I've lost it."

"A pity," she said. She was looking reproachfully at the neat arrangement of orange slices at the edge of my plate.

"It was part of a long story about how foods are changing," I told her. "In all the old European paintings the carrots used to be purple. Then some horticulturist fiddling around in his garden came up with an orange one, and it caught on."

"What about the flavor?" she asked.

"That's the other bad part. It didn't change."

"Well," she said, "carrots have been this color for a long time. You might as well get used to it."

"I'm sorry. I'm a traditionalist. It's like with tomatoes, which are supposed to be red. The yellow ones give me the creeps."

"When did I ever serve you yellow tomatoes?"

"Never," I said. "It's one of the things that has kept us together. In many ways I'm flexible, but I don't like people fooling around with my food."

"What other food are they fooling with?"

"Take turkeys, for example."

"The article mentioned turkeys?"

"I don't recall. But that just happens to be something I know quite a bit about. A lot of people think the turkey is hatched in a plastic wrapper with a wire around its legs. But that's not the case at all. Real turkeys don't look anything like what you get at the store."

"I'm listening."

"Real turkeys are long, narrow birds — fast runners, strong fliers. Then a government researcher came up with something called the Beltsville White. It's not really a turkey any more. The thing can't fly at all. It can hardly walk."

"It must make them easier to catch."

"That wasn't the point of it," I said. "He did it so people who are clumsy with knives could carve the bird without taking off a finger. And so dinner guests would say, '*Ooooh,* look at all that white meat.'"

"Is that so bad?"

"What's bad is when people mess with nature for purely commercial purposes. I don't think we ought to tinker with the global gene pool just to suit the grocery chains."

"Fine," said my wife, "but that still doesn't settle the question of your salad."

"I thought we'd passed on from that to other matters."

"Not a chance."

I looked down at the carrot slices, which still were the wrong color.

"The lettuce I can handle," I told her. "And red tomatoes. But not carrots. They sadden me, somehow."

"How will you get your fiber?"

"I will eat tree bark," I said. "There's no detectable difference."

"Have you never eaten carrots?"

"Of course. Cooked ones. When I was a boy, my mother made pot roast on Sunday. She put the carrots right in with the meat and potatoes. But that was different."

"Different how? Weren't they still orange?"

"Yes, but I didn't think of them as real food. They were just a vehicle to hold the grease."

The Polishing of Time

I have reached the stage in life when it is rather expected that a man will make himself ludicrous by his pursuit of much younger women.

Never mind his previous tastes, manners or a lifetime record of probity. Upon achieving a certain age, he is apt to begin affecting velour shirts unbuttoned to the navel and go prancing through the drive-ins on cloven hooves, ogling silky teen-age waitresses.

No one whom I know has ever actually done this. But the probability of it has become a part of the popular social mythology.

For myself, I can say truthfully that I am not much interested. The problem is not glandular. Nor do I mean any slight to those who have just passed from girlishness into the first full bloom of womanhood. Their freshness is engaging and they decorate the world. They have wonderful teeth. But the fact is that, as the years have passed, I have come to find more attraction — and more that is genuinely fascinating — in women who have lived long enough to display a moderate amount of weathering.

What has called this subject to mind is the fast approach of yet another birthday in these, the reputedly dangerous years. But what has helped clarify my feelings on the matter has been, oddly enough, a new-found amateur interest in the lapidary art — the search for beauty in stones.

On a trip recently we spent several hours gathering

pebbles along the shore of Lake Superior.

That region of our continent is especially ancient. By at least one geologist's account, it was among the first masses to be thrust above the primal, planetary sea. Suffice that those pebbles came from very old stock — just as, relatively speaking, do we.

There is no saying how long, how unimaginably long, they have been washing and shifting in those waters, little changed in any way except for some slight rounding over the millennia. Until finally they are rolled up to the margin and are picked from the water by some passer's hand — an event which, after all those ages, may be likened to a kind of birth.

Fresh from the water, they are wonderfully bright and varied in color. But that first attraction quickly fades. Let dry in the sun, they grow dull and disappointingly alike. A careful eye can detect certain blemishes and other character marks. But these suggest only faintly the virtue that might lie hidden inside the stone.

To discover it, one needs a machine called a tumbler.

The pebbles are put inside, many of them at once, and the barrel of the tumbler turns, driven by a small motor — endlessly, as the world turns, for weeks on end. In the barrel with the rocks are abrasive materials, grits whose textures vary with the hardness of the stone and the luster sought.

The process cannot be hurried. In revealing beauty, there is no substitute for time.

But when finally the pebbles are taken from the tumbler and cleaned, they are found to be lastingly transformed. Drying does not dull them any more. Their luster is permanent. Fractional layers have been ground away. So that what seemed, at the first, to be minor imperfections are accentuated and made clearer, becoming now lines and sworls arranged in patterns of considerable beauty. And the attraction is reliable; it will never change.

I see in this a possible explanation for the particular — the superior — appeal I find in women of a certain maturity and visible experience with life. We have been in the tumbler together and have been worked on by the grit that fills all our years. Layers have been worn away and our characters, for good or worse, are exposed the better to be seen.

I suppose it is possible that I may yet make a fool of myself, though I feel no hint of it coming on. Dogma and conventional humor hold that to be in the nature of older men. But I can say with fair confidence that it will never be over some bright trifle found glittering, untumbled and untested, in the deceptive shallows of a remembered youth.

MICKEY TAKES CHARGE

The pink cat, Mickey, likes to trifle with the bird dogs while they eat. It is not recommended behavior, since Pete and Bear regard mealtime as an occasion of profound seriousness.

They look through the back door glass until they see me appear from the basement with their filled bowls. Then great joy overtakes them, and they do a kind of whirling dance until the door is opened. Meantime, the pink cat, hearing the rattle of food being portioned out, comes from wherever he's been to wait for them in the kitchen.

He weighs at most five pounds, they 40-some. In all other ways they are brave creatures, bold and tireless afield. In Mickey's presence, though, their alarm is pitiful to see.

The canned food is mixed with the dry, and the bowls are put down side by side. They begin to eat. Then Mickey advances to lie between them. He reaches out a paw to lightly touch Pete's nearest hind foot. The dog moves a bit to the side. The foot is touched again, provoking another retreat. Soon Pete is revolving around his food bowl like the Earth around the Sun.

It must amuse the little cat to find how slight an effort is required to set so large a beast in motion.

Sometimes he walks directly under the dog, causing Pete's chewing — possibly even his heart — to stop. Or he will shoulder close and press his cheek against the dog's, intending to share the ration. Finally, the pup just backs away in despair. He's hungry, but eating isn't worth the trouble and the risk.

So Mickey has to be picked up and carried to another room, allowing the dog to be nourished in order that he may lead the way to quail when autumn comes. Immediately the cat is back, though, turning his attention to Bear, who has a pricklier nature.

The cat moves forward one step at a time — just close enough to elicit a growl. Bear's tail is wagging, but the front end of him is making that unpleasant sound. Causing the growl is the whole point, of course. It confirms that Mickey has achieved exactly that proximity which will produce the greatest possible anxiety, without provoking a charge. He lies down precisely there, watching the dogs wolf down whatever of their breakfast is left.

Bear used to be a finicky eater, dawdling over his food, sometimes looking first at his bowl, then up at me, resentful as some peasant faced with another year of nothing but potatoes and cabbage.

But now Bear doesn't loiter.

Oddly, though, out of these dramas at the breakfast hour has come an understanding that, while not quite a friendship yet, is on the way to being one.

In the evenings, when food isn't the issue and all the various shapes and species of us are together in the bedroom — no great tension can be detected. Five-pound Mickey still can herd the pups around the room pretty much as he likes. If he decides to occupy a chair that one of them prefers to sleep in, there's no hope of reclaiming it.

The one who feels misused just whines piteously and

finds another place.

But otherwise there's a fair amount of nose-touching and strategic sniffing. It will not be very long, I think, before we find two of them sharing a chair. That will not happen with the older, larger cats. *You're dogs,* their manner says. *We're a different family of creatures, and we're all better off just keeping our distance.*

But little Mickey seems not to put much stock in such distinctions. He's breaking new ground — crossing lines, making new friends, which always entails a bit of risk. And courage makes all the difference.

IX

THE CORNER TURNED

We woke at a blue hour, the pups and I, and had a bit of breakfast. And then, as the day lightened, we left the cabin and set forth like liberated youngsters into the perfection of an early autumn morning.

There's a song by that name, "Early Autumn." And as we started our ramble the words of it played in my head — as I remember them, at any rate.

> *When an early autumn walks the land*
> *and chills the breeze,*
> *And touches with her hand*
> *the summer trees,*
> *Perhaps you'll understand*
> *what memories I own . . .*

The rest goes on to be a love song, but that first verse fit the moment well. Because such a day does set one rummaging through one's store of memories. Memories of other such mornings at the season's turn, and where you happened to be on those days, and in what company.

The sun at half past 7 o'clock was two fingers above the field's east wood line. The ghost half-moon was directly overhead in the cloudless sky.

There's a difference in the light this time of year, noticeable at all hours but most pronounced in early morning and late afternoon. It must have to do in some way with the changed inclination of the planet on its axis. The dew-heavy grass shines darkly, each blade edged with brilliance and distinct from every other. The leaves of the cottonwoods and the yellow birch reflect like mirrors.

Where open ground gives way to forest, the shadows are deeper now than in any other season. A piece of woodland known for 30 years seems strangely unfamiliar.

In the wire of an old fence, I found a vine of bittersweet, and picked a bouquet of it for the one who had to be another place this day. There'd been a rain several days before, and in the dried mud of a track at the field's edge many deer had left their hoofprints. And in a chest-high growth of weeds were the pressed-down ovals where they'd bedded.

The pups, Pete and Bear, crossed the big field, the middle one, and turned up the derelict fencerow, overgrown with wild rose and blackberry canes and thickets of plum. They passed the place where their father rests under a pile of stones, though of course they couldn't know it. In less than a month we'll visit that place again, and I expect his pups will find the quail coveyed there, as Rufus and I so often did. For now, the world is too rank with greenery. It will take a hard frost, or more likely several, to burn back the vegetation enough that scenting will be possible. But work was not the point of our outing, anyway.

Sometimes I trudged along behind. Other times I just stood, on a rise where the view was open, and watched the joyful flight of them to the far end of seeing. Always, though, the sound of the whistle would bring them back. And returning from a last, long cast they were content finally to take their ease, get an ear scratched and wolf down the biscuits I'd brought in my pocket.

Their coats were wet, and matted with clinging seeds. Their eyes were red from plunging headlong through the thorniest tangles. Their happiness, in short, was complete. The sun was fully risen, the day quickly warming. We sat together in the damp grass by the car. I was imagining forward to hunts already planned. Their heads were raised, noses searching for those tomorrows on the breeze.

There's no season I love as passionately as this one, and nowhere else I'd as soon greet it.

"So it's begun!" I told the pups, who turned to look at me with golden eyes, not understanding the words but knowing something of importance was near at hand.

IT'S BEARABLE SHAME

I just can't keep that woman out of the yard.

She's out there again, leaf rake in hand, humiliating me in front of the neighbors, all of whom hire teams of men with mechanical blowers or order their minor children to collect up the leaves.

Please do not think I am lazy. *Cheap*, maybe, but not lazy. There is nothing I would rather do than spend the next month or so tidying up the grounds. In fact, when we moved here, the lawn was my governing passion. The man before me had a gift for growing grass. Probably he fertilized. The result was a vigorous green turf, whose blades stood stiff and straight as a Marine's crewcut.

But after our first year or two in the house, the slippage began.

My lawn mower broke — the one passed down from my wife's father. The grass became discouraged by lack of feeding, and gave way first to weeds, then to beaten earth. That's how it's been for years now. Leaves, however, we still have in great quantity. And, as I've said, there is nothing I would rather do than deal with them myself.

Unfortunately, my time is quite valuable and I have a great many obligations. So it simply is not feasible that I should be expected to rake the yard. If it were left to me, I would let nature have its way. For one thing, there will be winds. Always in autumn there are winds. They tend to blow in from a westerly direction. In due course, our leaves would become the property of neighbors to the east.

The few left behind we could classify as mulch, or eventually as compost. Slow decay would return them to the soil to nourish new growth. That is the normal cycle of living things. That the environmentally sound approach also happens to be the easy one is entirely coincidental. It simply was not in Nature's grand plan that the glory of the autumn should be turned into a burden and a torment.

The sensible course, then, is to let time handle things. By spring, the leaves will be forgotten. Or if not this next spring, certainly in a couple of years.

That's my view of it. But no! My wife insists on presenting herself out there in full view of everyone on the street — the leaf martyr, the Joan of Arc of autumn with a rake for a sword. If I had wanted to share life with a woman with calluses on her hands, I'd have married a Russian beet-picker.

Meantime I sit inside here, husbanding my valuable time, meeting important obligations, watching her toil away in a pathetic bid for sympathy. I know what other people must think of me, and the shame I feel is rather great.

But it is bearable.

PHIL NEVER MAKES ME CRY

No man I know would submit willingly, regularly and at a fancy price to an ordeal almost sure to leave him emotionally shattered and sunk in humiliation. Which is why men cannot understand women's dealings with their hair-dressers.

I realize I'm treading, here, on delicate terrain. But against the charge of sexism, as against the charge of libel, truth is the sovereign defense.

Men do not go to the barbershop to *find* themselves — to have their personalities revealed, as Michelangelo liberated the statue of David from its prison in a block of stone. They mean simply to get their hair cut. The preliminaries are few and to the point.

"Same way?"

"Yeah, the same."

"Kind of short in the back and full on the sides, right?"

"Right. Same way."

The matter is settled. Talk turns to more interesting things. The barber's chair is a pleasant interlude. One hears good jokes there, most of them unrepeatable here. Men are not vain about their hair. They ask only to be sent out in some presentable state, looking — for good or ill — about as they've always looked.

I enjoy my barber, Phil, a lot. He is a working man, like all the rest of us. He does an honest job for an honest dollar. He tells good stories. He is reported to be a powerful third baseman in the softball leagues, and I can say from experience that his tennis forehand is very strong. He does not, I am sure, regard himself as some kind of *artiste*. Or see my head as a blank canvas upon which to express the caprices of his imagination.

"About the same?" he says.

"The same," I reply. And we have a perfect understanding. His scissors go snickety-snick. He tells about having a run of luck at a blackjack table in Las Vegas. Maybe we make a tennis date.

"Next," he says.

And I go away content.

Not so the women of my family, or, I suspect, of yours. For them, the visit to the hair-dresser is an event freighted with danger and great suspense. They go there for adventure. Often as not, they come away in tears.

"Be honest," my daughter implored after a recent styling. "Does it look like me?"

"Sure," I answered honestly. "It looks like you with all your hair cut off. What happened? Did you go to sleep in the chair?"

"I told him what I wanted," she groaned. "But *this* is what he did."

"Did you pay him?"

"Yes," she said desolately. "A lot." And went off to grieve in privacy.

I have heard of certain very wealthy women who spend part of every day at the beauty salon. My heart goes out to them. That is more unhappiness than even the rich should have to bear.

Scientists pour their failed experiments down the laboratory drain. Hair stylists send theirs out to the dance. Phil, my barber, is a model of consistency. He may have booted a ball or two at third base, but in the shop he never has a bad day.

DEAD MAN WRITING

A reader called the other day to comment on a piece of mine that had appeared in his morning paper. My wife answered the phone. The caller said he followed the column regularly and often passed it along to friends. But he had a question.

"I was talking about it with this man I know, and the fellow said, 'Oh, he's dead. Somebody else is writing that stuff now.'"

There was a momentary silence.

"Well?" said the caller.

"Just a moment," my wife told him. She covered the mouthpiece of the phone.

"The man wants to know if you're dead."

"How should I know?"

"No," she told him. "There seems to be a pulse."

In that case, the caller said, he would be pleased if she would pass on his regards. Which she did.

Writing is a lonely business, and it's always nice to get feedback on your work. But the man's question was troubling. How widely, I wondered, had the news of my death circulated. Rumors like that need to be squelched right at the start. Because once they get a little currency they can be hard to stop.

I can imagine, for instance, a meeting at the newspaper where the editors and top executives would be discussing staff compensation for the year ahead. They would come to my name on the list.

"You mean we're still paying him?" the publisher would say. "I thought he was dead."

"You could be right, sir. We haven't seen him in a while."

"Notify payroll."

"Yes, sir."

"And find out who's writing that column. We'll need a new picture. I don't want a dead man's face in the paper three times a week."

Official-looking documents will arrive in the mail from the probate court. My credit cards will be canceled. My old college will send a representative to ask about obtaining the shoe box full of my priceless papers, and various organizations will solicit my wife for donation of my clothes.

The thing will get a life of its own.

Relatives I've never even heard of will appear with their attorneys, demanding to see copies of the will. Before it's over, so many people will have a stake in this that there'll be no choice but to have a friend drive me to the airport — very slowly, in my Bronco — and fly off to Belize or somewhere to live out my years under an assumed name.

I will say this, though. The hard part of writing a column is keeping the language vigorous and the quality more or less consistent from day to day.

Having readers think you're dead takes a lot of the pressure off.

ONE MAN'S SONG

It was a Saturday morning, with few pedestrians abroad and little traffic moving on the street in the business district.

I could hear his song when he still was a block away.

Down the slant of sidewalk came the small figure — past the building fronts and the locked doorways. He walked with such a bounce that I took him for a youngster. His melody preceded him. Some kind of gospel song, it was, flung skyward in a tone as pure and sweet as the voices of the Vienna Boys' Choir.

That street can be uninviting, a little threatening, on a day when car and foot traffic is light. Loiterers with predatory eyes lean against the outer wall of the convenience store across the way. Panhandlers and drunks come lurching.

You avoid eye contact, and let them pass.

I was loading a carton, and had to make room for it in the back of the car. By the time I closed the trunk lid, the singer had nearly drawn abreast. I could see then he was no boy. He was a black man in his 30s, in T-shirt, jeans and tennis shoes. Though short of stature, he looked fit as someone who'd spent a lot of time lifting weights.

It really didn't consciously cross my mind to speak to him. That's just not something you do in these uneasy and polemical times, when anger is abroad, violence can erupt without reason, and our differences define us.

He and I were men of different ages, different races, different experience and very possibly different luck. Let this stranger walk on by, good sense told me. But, then, quite unbidden, the words just came out.

"That's a wonderful voice I hear."

He stopped and turned — a little startled, I believe. Then his face exploded in a smile so full of appreciation and frank good will that the imagined distance between us instantly disappeared.

"Thank you," he said. "I'm glad you like it."

And he continued on down the walk, his step light, his music filling the street.

I didn't get in my car and drive immediately away. I waited until he passed into the next block and out of hearing, not wanting to miss a single note.

It was such a small incident, perhaps, as hardly to be worth telling here. I was struck, though, by the thought that, at that very moment, there were people — not just in this country, but the world over — sharpening their knives, oiling their guns, and planning mischief against other people who happen to be in some way unlike themselves.

All in the name of their differences — though the differences amount to so little, after all.

Odd, isn't it, how one man's song can lift and change the day?